ENDORSEMENTS

"If you want to dig deeper into the scriptures this book is for you. The author shares his own experience of walking with God via the Word of God. He talks about how awesome our God is, how God sees us as His children, how to listen to and hear the voice of God, learning both the wisdom and the knowledge of God, how to enter into the Kingdom of God and how to live under the guidance of the Holy Spirit. Much more is covered in this book which brings the Holy Scriptures alive in our life.

God *wants* to speak to you. Yet many Christians struggle to hear God voice for themselves. Ron Heyn's book, "*I Gave You My Word*" focuses not only hearing God through his written word but provides very practical examples of hearing the rhema or "now" word of God for your life through real-life experiences. This book sheds light on how God speaks to us in and through everyday circumstances and how we can apply God's personal direction to our lives.

—Tom Schissel, friend of the author

I'd like to say that this book *I Gave You My Word* has been for me a great guide to making the Bible relevant and alive in the world today. It is no longer just words on a page but those words become real, alive and dynamic possibilities in my life. Thank you for such important insights to something I have heard and read all my life."

—Nancy Thorson, friend of the author

"I Gave You My Word is filled with beautiful Scripture that Ron experienced coming ALIVE in his life! God speaks so tenderly and clearly with encouragement, healing and hope. This book gives a deeper understanding of God's Word in down to earth language, with the focus on THANKSGIVING for everything He, in His love, provides for us! It gives the reader a wonderful chance to get to know Him better. He gave us His Word...discover how faithful He is!"

—Robin Hafey, friend of the author

I Gave You My
WORD

I Gave You My
WORD

A simple way to understand the power of God's word

Ron Heyn

I Gave You My Word: A Simple Way To Understand The Power Of God's Word

Copyright © 2022 by Ron Heyn

All rights reserved. No part of this publication may be reproduced, distributed, or transmitted in any form or by any means, including photocopying, recording, or other electronic or mechanical methods, without the prior written permission of the publisher, except in the case of brief quotations embodied in critical reviews and certain other non-commercial uses permitted by copyright law.

Jones Media Publishing
10645 N. Tatum Blvd. Ste. 200-166
Phoenix, AZ 85028
www.JonesMediaPublishing.com

Disclaimer:

The author strives to be as accurate and complete as possible in the creation of this book, notwithstanding the fact that he does not warrant or represent at any time that the contents within are accurate due to the rapidly changing nature of the Internet.

While all attempts have been made to verify information provided in this publication, the Publisher assumes no responsibility for errors, omissions, or contrary interpretation of the subject matter herein. Any perceived slights of specific persons, peoples, or organizations are unintentional.

In practical advice books, like anything else in life, there are no guarantees of income made. Readers are cautioned to reply on their own judgment about their individual circumstances to act accordingly. This book is not intended for use as a source of legal, business, accounting or financial advice. All readers are advised to seek services of competent professionals in legal, business, accounting, and finance field.

ISBN: 978-1-948382-40-3 paperback

Printed in the United States of America

TABLE OF CONTENTS

Acknowledgements............................ix

Introduction xi

Chapter 1: The Original Motivation Behind Writing This Book............................1

Chapter 2: The Lifegiving Nature of God's Word ... 7

Chapter 3: Understanding Our Identity Through Christ................................15

Chapter 4: We Have an Awesome God........... 27

Chapter 5: The Spirit or The Flesh 41

Chapter 6: What Is Faith? 53

Chapter 7: Hearing God Speak 65

Chapter 8: Missing God's Command 81

Chapter 9: Discerning God's Will 87

Chapter 10: Baptism of the Holy Spirit.......... 103

Chapter 11: Where Did the Power Go?.......... 109

Chapter 12: Confronting Evil 117

Chapter 13: When I am Weak is When I am
             Strong 137

Chapter 14: We Apparently Have Two Angels 145

Chapter 15: Let He Who Is Without Sin Cast
             the First Stone 151

Chapter 16: The Truth Will Set You Free 155

Chapter 17: Making Vows 159

Chapter 18: Honor Father and Mother 165

Chapter 19: Rejoice Always 171

Chapter 20: Where Do You Live 179

Chapter 21: Seek Me First 189

Chapter 22: Sorrow - A Key Ingredient to
             Repentance 197

Chapter 23: Wake Up Church 203

About The Author 207

Appendix A: Scripture References by Chapter . . . 209

ACKNOWLEDGEMENTS

I would like to thank a host of people who have helped me with this book. I had lots of people read various drafts and if I omitted your name, it was clearly a mistake on my part.

First, I would like to thank Reverend Al Kurz, a resident in the community where my wife and I now live. Extremely helpful in pointing me toward a number of scriptures, Al listened to my ideas and offered great encouragement as I wrote this book.

I also need to thank my very close friend, Tom Schissel. Tom has graciously labored reading my various drafts, providing input on what to include and how to express it.

I also need to thank my wife, Anita, for being a sounding board and for correcting my grammar and for her patience as I spent many hours at my desk writing. Thank you to Brenda Theilen for her sharp eye in finding many initial errors. I also received editing help from a number of people including Dr Mark Zachary, Kerran Pettit, Joan West, Robin Hafey, and Nancy and Ken Thorenson. All of the above people gave me extremely encouraging feedback.

Finally, I want to thank my publisher, Jeremy Jones, who has not only been encouraging as he has led me through the steps required to complete this book, but his professional manner made it easy and delightful to work with him.

Note: All scripture references are taken from the New American Bible Revised Edition unless otherwise noted.

INTRODUCTION

When I began to think about writing this book, in the back of my mind, I thought the entire book should be about the power of the Word of God. I reached a point where I just could not get enough thoughts to begin writing. Consequently, after spending a lot of time trying to organize my thoughts – and I am talking about months and months – I finally changed the focus.

It was during this initial attempt, after asking God for help, that the title of the book seemed to jump off the pages of the Bible. I believe He told me that title was to be "I Gave You My Word." I have to tell you I am not comfortable writing where the title implies God is actually writing this. On the other hand, I believe God wants us to know Him through the Word He gave us. The best way I can describe it is that I believe the Holy Spirit is inspiring the contents of this book.

I come from a Roman Catholic background. Consequently, a number of the examples I write about refer to things related to that background. However, the intent of this book is to focus on God's word and not a particular religious bent. I believe that the writings expressed in the following pages are applicable to all Christians.

Since I have no theology degree, nor do I claim to know the scriptures inside out, I write from the experiences I've had in my relationship with God. The reader should focus on the presence and power of the Holy Spirit in the examples, as I do not claim to be "special." As you read the scripture references, I suggest you read them for how each scripture passage speaks to you personally. Not every scripture will evoke a personal message. I once attended a conference where the speaker referred to the following scriptures from Matthew 13:44-46:

44 "The kingdom of heaven is like a treasure buried in a field, which a person finds and hides again, and out of joy goes and sells all that he has and buys that field. 45 Again, the kingdom of heaven is like a merchant searching for fine pearls. 46 When he finds a pearl of great price, he goes and sells all that he has and buys it."

The speaker said that when you are reading the scriptures, and a particular scripture evokes a prompting, think of that scripture as described in verses 44-46. Sell out for it. Pray about it and let the Holy Spirit lead you. The scriptures should be read with a deep hunger for a relationship with God. In other words, read the scriptures looking for that treasure, that pearl of great price.

A few years ago, while attending a week-long revival, a friend suggested I see a Prophetic Ministry team as they were praying over people. I was not even sure what it meant to have someone pray over me with regards to the prophetic nor did I have any idea what to expect. When I sat down to be prayed over, the person who seemed to be leading the ministry said something to the effect that I possessed much wisdom and knowledge that people needed to hear. She went on to say that this wisdom and knowledge did not come so much from my knowledge of scripture, but rather that God had been tutoring me. This statement blew me away; there was so much truth to it. I had gone through a lot of healing while recovering from depression and, later, as I was led into a healing ministry, it was during those times God often described to me or explained to me that which had taken place. Later in the prophetic prayer time the same person told me I was one of God's Oracles; He used me to speak specific messages to people I was praying over. I didn't even know what the term "Oracle" meant but I do know there were times when I was praying over someone that I spoke a message that did not come from my mind, but in every case what I said seemed to profoundly touch the recipient. I was learning that it was the Holy Spirit speaking through me.

Simply stated, God is longing for us to have a personal and intimate relationship with Him. His Word clearly points this out. He sent His only Son to reconcile our relationship with Him. The ball has been placed in our hands as to whether or not we will respond to that invitation. My hope is that the contents of this book will bring the reader into a closer personal relationship with God. At the very least, my hope is that by reading this book the reader will want to pursue such a relationship with God.

The whole notion about a relationship with Him was once very foreign to me. I thought I had to be "good," go to church and follow the guidelines the church had set up for me to get into heaven. I did not even begin to scratch the surface of the notion of God steering my life in a very personal way. It was not until years later I looked back and saw God had been guiding my life and I didn't even know it. Once I became a teenager, I hardly gave God much thought. I was too busy running my own life.

In 1976, my wife and I attended a marriage retreat called the "Marriage Encounter Weekend." On this particular weekend, we both heard the Holy Spirit call us to change our lives. This happened despite the fact that we were in separate rooms when we heard the message. We said yes to the call as best we could while still working full time and while raising four children. I write about experiences I (we) had with regards to working under the guidance of the Holy Spirit.

I can be a little slow on the intake, but I began to see that God has given us His promise, which is expressed through the Word: The Holy Scriptures. Furthermore, the first chapter of the Gospel of John tells us that Jesus is the Word of God made flesh. He gave us His Word. He gave us Jesus.

CHAPTER 1

THE ORIGINAL MOTIVATION BEHIND WRITING THIS BOOK

Several experiences in life played a large role in driving my desire to write this book. I will share these experiences to, hopefully, grab your attention; these experiences come from direct and personal encounters with the Spirit of God. My hope is that I can describe those experiences so as to affect the reader to desire a deeper relationship with God (the Holy Spirit) in his or her own life.

Before I talk about some experiences of the power of God's word, let me pose the following scripture from the book of Hebrews 4:12:

*[12] Indeed, **the word of God is living and effective, sharper than any two-edged sword**, penetrating even between soul and spirit, joints and marrow, **and***

able to discern reflections and thoughts of the heart.

That is a pretty strong message about the Word of God. The first point is the Word of God is not a story book nor is it an account of things that occurred throughout time. The Word of God is living, which means it is alive today– and as we read the Word of God, it can actually speak to us and can direct our lives, etc.

At one point in my life, I had promised God I would read the entire Bible. Not only am I a slow reader but my reading comprehension isn't that strong. Despite this, I diligently read at least one chapter a day and three on Sundays. When I got to the last book of the Bible, the book of Revelation, I fell asleep each day as I tried to read it. I finally gave up. When I was in the middle of trying to recover from depression, while praying, I heard in my spirit that God wanted me to read the book of Revelation. This time when I read it, I could not put it down. As I read, one message in particular jumped off the pages. That message was: the heavenly hosts were praising God. I realized God was calling me to enter into the practice of praising him every day and throughout the day, for that matter. In fact, the first thing I do when I awaken is to praise God. This is true even when I wake up in the middle of the night. It is amazing how that action helped to lift the depression I'd found myself in. A year or two later, again while praying, I heard in my spirit that I was to read the book of Revelation again. This time when I read it, all I heard in my spirit was the call to repentance. I spent some time writing down all the sins from my past life that I could remember and then called a priest to hear my confession. The Word of God is indeed a living message.

Many years ago, I attended a talk presented by Father John Hampsch, CMF (Claretian Missionary Father). The talk was about the power of God's Word. I wish I had recorded the talk because it had a profound effect on me. I believe it was one of the things that caused me to delve deeper into the Word of God, something I was not accustomed to doing. I do remember Father Hampsch talking about a meeting he had attended in which people from many faiths were present. The speaker was an ordained minister who happened to be speaking about the same subject: the Power of God's Word. In his talk, the speaker referenced a section of the Old Testament that he said seemed to be quite boring and seemingly unrelatable. The speaker went on to say that even that part of God's Word had the power to change lives. Father Hampsch said as this minister preached on these particular verses, the

Holy Spirit seemed to come over the room. Before he knew it, everyone in the room ended up lying face down, repenting and worshiping God.

Another time, I was listening to a tape created by a friend who said that while he was holding a healing service one evening, and while he was praying with people as they came forward for prayer, one person approached him. This person desperately asked for prayers for their child who was apparently very ill. My friend received a word of knowledge indicating the person asking for prayers was actually a worshiper of Satan. My friend told the person he would not pray but that the person needed to give up the worship of Satan and turn to Christ. The person left very upset.

When my friend and his wife were closing up and locking the doors of the church where they had held the healing service, the same person came out of the shadows in a state of despair begging my friend to pray for their child. My friend reached out to this person apparently to pray while at the same time my friend's wife flipped open the Bible and began to read the Word of God. The person seeking prayer (the Satan worshiper) fell to the ground and tried to cover her ears while screaming something like, "No, not the Word of God. Get away from me!"

The passages my friend's wife read were from the first chapter of the book of Matthew, which is about the lineage of Christ's family history. Evidently, the Power of the Word caused this person to cry out and repent of her Satanic worship and to say, in effect, that she wanted to turn their life to Christ. The person's child was apparently healed at that very hour. Notice how the Word of God being read penetrated the heart of the Satan worshiper and brought about a conversion of heart. I wonder if the Word of God is more effective for the recipient when the recipient is in a state of desiring a deeper relationship with God or at the very least is seeking God's power to change something in their lives that they cannot change themselves. Keep that in mind as you read the rest of this book. I have been told that worshipers of Satan are very aware of the power of God and of God's Word. I am not so sure that Christian church-goers have that same depth of awareness.

I myself experienced the power of God's Word in a profound way while my wife and I were in our den praying for a married couple that had come to us for counseling and healing. While we were praying over them, I began to speak the message of the scripture from Philippians 2:5-11.

In that scripture we are told that Jesus emptied himself and humbled himself, becoming obedient even to the point of death on the cross. Because of this, God exalted Him, giving Him the name above all other names and that at the name of Jesus every knee will bend, whether in heaven or on earth and under the earth and every tongue will confess that Jesus is Lord, to the Glory of God the Father.

As I continued to pray these words from the scriptures, the atmosphere in our family room changed as though the angels of heaven were present. The couple for whom we were praying wept and were apparently healed of whatever problems they were dealing with. Why things unfolded that way, I have no idea, but it seemed to me that God's power manifested through the Word that was being proclaimed.

CHAPTER 2

THE LIFEGIVING NATURE OF GOD'S WORD

I don't know about you, but I always saw myself in the physical realm. While I know we are more than that —we are both body and spirit – I never really got past me as the person who was 10 lbs. 2 oz. at birth, I was very aware that I was usually bigger than children my age, I grew to be 6'6" tall etc. While I knew my physical body would be left behind to be disposed of (buried or cremated) and my spirit would move on when I died – hopefully to heaven and not the other place – I really did not understand anything about my spirit. Consequently, some of the scriptures did not really connect the dots for me.

In both the old and new testaments, we are told that the Word of God gives us life. In the Deuteronomy 8:3 the word tells us:

*³ He therefore let you be afflicted with hunger, and then fed you with manna, a food unknown to you and your ancestors, **so you might know that it is not by bread alone that people live, but by all that comes forth from the mouth of the LORD.***

In the Gospel of Matthew 4:4 the Word tells us the following:

*⁴ He said in reply, "It is written: **'One does not live by bread alone, but by every word that comes forth from the mouth of God.'"***

In Luke 4:4 the same message is given, namely:

*⁴ But Jesus answered him saying, "It is written, **'Man shall not live by bread alone, but by every word of God.'"***

These three scripture verses tell us the Word of God feeds our spirit whereas the bread feeds our body. When we don't eat bread (food) and allow our body to process that food, our body slowly dies. When we don't take in the Word of God and process the Word, our spirit becomes listless and, eventually, we cut ourselves off from our relationship with God. I'll discuss processing the Word of God later in the book.

The book of Proverbs 14:12 and Proverbs 16:25 tells us the following:

²⁵ *There is a way that seems right to a man, but its end is the way to death.* (New King James Version (NKJV)).

The New American Bible (NAB) essentially states the same thing, namely:

²⁵ Sometimes a way seems right, but the end of it leads to death.

We have been taught that if we work hard, and stick with it, we can do anything. We spend most of our lives, and certainly our work lives, applying this mentality to all things we face in life. We tend to focus on the spiritual when we go to church on Sunday's, if at all. We tend to think that being spiritual is for priests, deacons, ministers and nuns. For many of us, it is only when we run into hard times, things like sickness, money problems, family or other relationship problems, and don't seem to have any alternatives that we turn to God.

The result is that we tend to starve our spirits. Thus, we ever so slowly separate ourselves from God and from the intimate relationship He desires to have with us. I don't believe God separates himself from us. Since we have free will, it must be like having a friendship with someone, but we slowly walk away from the friendship. For some, it leaves us believing our friend will never take us back so we don't even try. For others, we never look back and we just leave and forget we ever had that friendship in the first place.

I firmly believe that if we really knew what having a relationship with God meant as far as having a peaceful and joyful life, we would do everything we could to stay close in that relationship. In order to have a close relationship with someone, we have to be able to communicate with that person. This means we must have a way to convey what we are thinking and experiencing (usually through talking to that person) and we must have a way of listening to and hearing what that person wishes to convey to us.

I was raised in the Lutheran Church. In my younger years, we lived in a suburban community on Long Island just outside of Manhattan. I attended church with my family almost every Sunday. Our pastor was a wonderful man and I can remember learning a lot about Christ through the scriptures. Deep down, I believed Jesus not only healed people when He walked the earth but that he could and would still heal people now. What I don't remember was any discussion in my family or even around me about how to incorporate Christ into our everyday lives, other than trying not to sin, being nice to other people, and, of course, by attending church every Sunday. In other words, we were to apply the Golden Rule, to treat others in the same way we would like to be treated.

As far as going to church goes, I remember trying to listen very attentively to whoever was preaching and, if I liked what they had said, I tried to live out the message. Oftentimes, that intention seemed to disappear before the week was over. The fact of the matter was that what was preached in church was seldom lived out by most people in my world. People seemed to go to church because they felt better when they did. Others attended, especially teens, because they were told they had to do so. Others seemed to attend church for the social aspects associated with the members of that church. The list goes on. I just do not remember many people talking about worshiping God and how God was present in their lives.

When I was 11 going on 12, our family moved to a dairy farm in upstate New York. The nearest Lutheran church was about 12 miles away. My mother did not drive. My brother was already confirmed a few years before and my mother wanted me to be confirmed as well. Because we were on a dairy farm, it took a lot of effort and commitment to finish chores on a Sunday morning, get cleaned up (we did not have a shower, just a bathtub), and get changed into the proper clothes for church.

When we went to church, I was embarrassed because my father and my brother often fell asleep during the service. After the service, I had to attend classes to prepare for confirmation while my family waited for me. There was, to say the least, a lot of tension and lack of patience within my family during these times. I eventually finished my classes and was confirmed. We never went back to church after that. The notion of God slowly slipped away from me except for the fact that my mother had given me a wallet sized picture of Christ that said, "I am with you always" under the picture. Every so often, when I was alone, I would look at the picture and say to myself that I was not worthy of being His follower. The frequency of even looking at the picture became less and less over time. I could easily say I no longer had a relationship with God; in fact, I was just about spiritually dead.

What happens when we make our decisions without taking God and His ways into account is that we become very self-sufficient. That tends to make us less dependent on God and, over time, God is placed in the "back seat" or perhaps just not a part of our lives at all.

It is a good thing God does not interact with us in that way. It was only years later that I could look back in my life and realize He was not only calling me to a relationship with Him but that many things in my life that had occurred in the past were driven by the living God. I will talk about some of those things in later chapters. We will also look at what the scriptures tell us when we not only read the Word, but make living by the Word our normal way of life that God is clearly blessing us with.

I have since entered into a more personal relationship with God that has changed my whole view of God and my role in that relationship.

CHAPTER 3

UNDERSTANDING OUR IDENTITY THROUGH CHRIST

I never really understood who I am to God. I said the words, "God the Father" and thought of God as a Father but I never embraced God as being my Father on a personal level. It was more like something we said and talked about to some degree, but never from an awareness that I am not only God's adopted son but that He had actually created me. Furthermore, I had no idea that God knew me before the foundation of the world (Ephesians 1:4). I think the fact that we referred to Jesus as God's only begotten Son in some ways supported that view. When we recite the Lord's prayer, it starts with, "Our Father who art in heaven." This alone left me wondering if He is really my personal father; He is never around. Growing up, my earthly father was around (when he wasn't working). In my case, my earthly father tucked me into bed virtually every night, brushing his hand through my hair, telling me he loved me and kissing me good night. This continued right up through my high school years. Furthermore, I can honestly say that, despite the fact that the Word of God tells me that God created me, it never entered my mind.

In Romans 8:14-16 the Bible tells us the following:

***14 For those who are led by the Spirit of God are children of God. 15 For you did not receive a spirit of slavery to fall back into fear, but you received a spirit of adoption, through which we cry, "Abba,* Father!"** 16 The Spirit itself bears witness with our spirit that we are children of God.*

In Galatians 3:26 we are told:

26 For through faith you are all children of God in Christ Jesus.

These scriptures are pretty clear. That being said, since I had a relatively small knowledge of the scriptures, those two particular verses were never in the conscious part of my thinking.

What was more prevalent in my thinking was my sinfulness and whether or not I was really good enough to make it into heaven. I was never well disciplined in my behavior so I always had some doubt as to whether or not I was "qualified" to be a Christian. I think, for me at least, that subject overshadowed and kind of blotted out the idea of really being a child of God.

Consequently, I believe one of the most important subjects necessary to understanding our identity in Christ is whether or not we're saved "by works" (our efforts to be good enough to be saved) or saved "by grace."

In the mid-90s, my wife and I were part of a small group of married couples who were meeting regularly to pray and to share our walk with God. We were all of the Catholic faith. Some had been Catholic since their infant baptism while others, like me, chose to be part of the Catholic family as adults. In my case, the reason to go back to church and become Catholic was to bridge a gap in my marriage. Furthermore, each of the couples had had a powerful experience on a Marriage Encounter Weekend and we all had followed that with attending a Life in the Spirit seminar and had been baptized in the Holy Spirit. The subject of "saved by works or saved by grace" came up and we had to admit we were not familiar enough with the scriptures regarding this subject. Consequently, we invited a friend, who was an Ordained Minister in a Bible-based church, to teach us about the scriptures regarding the subject.

Learning what was actually written in the scriptures was a very painful experience because what the scriptures revealed was in direct conflict with what we had been taught in our church. I have no specific memory about this subject from my childhood days as a Lutheran. I do remember discussions about it with friends after I had joined the Catholic Church. I remember thinking, "Why are we even discussing this subject?" It did not seem very important to me in my new walk as a church-goer.

The scriptures clearly state that salvation comes from God. It is a gift, given to man, by God. There is nothing we can do to earn salvation. This fact turned everything around for me.

For example, Ephesians 2:4-9 tells us:

***4** **But God, who is rich in mercy, because of the great love he had for us,** **5** **even when we were dead in our transgressions, brought us to life with Christ (by grace you have been saved)**, **6** raised us up with him, and seated us with him in the heavens in Christ Jesus, **7** that in the ages to come he might show the immeasurable riches of his grace in his kindness to us in Christ Jesus. **8 For by grace you have been saved through faith**, and this is not from you; it is the gift of God; **9 it is not from works**, so no one may boast.*

God loves us so much that His mercy is extended to us even though we are sinners. He does this as a gift. The scripture tells us **we must believe** it in order to receive the gift. The gift is that we are saved by grace through faith.

Let me divert just a bit to talk about faith. I do this because I have used and heard the word faith to mean various things. In the second chapter of the book of James, the writer tells us faith without works is useless. The referenced "works" is living what you have faith in. It is not a head trip. So, when you have faith that you have been saved, you will live like you've been saved. This means that the part about works in Ephesians 2 verse 9, above, is not referring to the notion that I must be good enough to earn being saved. When I approach salvation with that mentality, I am driven to do good things with the hope of going to heaven. That mentality of the meaning of works is in direct conflict with being saved by grace (not by works). The meaning is more like...from your salvation, good works naturally follow.

I don't think it gets much clearer than that.

What I discovered that summer while studying the scriptures, specifically dealing with this subject that seemed to contradict what had been a "truth" and that had been a fabric of my life, was that accepting the "new" truth can be very difficult to handle. I found that at times my whole body seemed to reject it; it was hard to not be angry with the messenger. I bring this up just in case you experience the same kind of response.

Because the scripture I referenced above was so very clear, I could not reject it. Consequently, I found I could not walk away from this "new truth" but, rather, was compelled to continue processing it. In the beginning, the process we were going through left me confused. When I began to see how clear it was in the scriptures that we are definitely saved by God's grace, I had to deal with a sense that I had been misled for most of my life.

I performed a search for the word "salvation" and found 153 such references in the Bible I was using. Here are a few examples:

Exodus 15:2

*² My strength and my refuge is the LORD, **and he has become my savior.** This is my God, I praise him; the God of my father, I extol him.*

2 Samuel 22:3

*³ my God, my rock of refuge! My shield, my saving horn, my stronghold, my refuge, **my savior**, from violence you keep me safe.*

2 Samuel 22:47

*⁴⁷ The LORD lives! Blessed be my rock! Exalted be God, the **rock of my salvation.***

Psalms 13:6

*⁶ But I trust in your mercy. Grant my heart **joy in your salvation**, I will sing to the LORD, for he has dealt bountifully with me.*

Psalms 62:7

God alone is my rock and my salvation, my fortress; I shall not fall.

Micah 7:7

*⁷ But as for me, I will look to the LORD, **I will wait for God my savior;** my God will hear me.*

Luke 3:5-6

*⁵ Every valley shall be filled and every mountain and hill shall be made low. The winding roads shall be made straight, and the rough ways made smooth, ⁶ **and all flesh shall see the salvation of God.***

Ephesians 1:13

*¹³ In him you also**, who have heard the word of truth, the gospel of your salvation, and***

have believed in him, were sealed with the promised holy Spirit.

1 Peter 1:8-9

[8] Although you have not seen him you love him; even though you do not see him now yet believe in him, you rejoice with an indescribable and glorious joy, [9] ***as you attain the goal of [your] faith, the salvation of your souls.***

Revelation 19:1

[1] After this I heard what sounded like the loud voice of a great multitude in heaven, saying: "Alleluia! ***Salvation, glory, and might belong to our God.***

Incidentally, in case you did not recognize it, this "new truth" was one of the points made by Martin Luther that led to the Protestant Reformation. In 1999, on Reformation Sunday, my wife and I were attending Mass at our Cathedral Parish, whereby our Bishop and the local Lutheran Bishop read some of the scriptures pertaining to this very subject; the Roman Catholic Church admitted they had erred and that Luther was right regarding this subject.

There are three reasons I bring this up. I found that as I absorbed this truth my spirituality changed because I saw my relationship with God differently. In my eyes, God became more of a friend and my Father. He became a loving Father and I knew I would spend my eternity in Heaven. This is my gift which was given to me by God! That is awesome! My part in this is to believe it.

Secondly, I cannot remember any teachings/discussions presented by the hierarchy of the church to explain what this means to a person's relationship with God. While attending a meeting, recently, one man did say he was taught in Catholic school that we are saved by grace. I think this point is extremely important to call attention to because of how it can radically affect a person's relationship with God, as well as their view of God.

In addition to what I talked about above, the third reason is that learning this truth and incorporating it into my life had a very positive effect on my relationship with members of other faiths. Why is this important? In the Gospel of John, in the 17th chapter, Jesus is praying to the Father on the night before he was to be crucified. In verses 20 and 21 it says:

[20] *"I pray not only for them, but also for those who will believe in me through their word,* [21] ***so that they may all be one, as you, Father, are in me***

and I in you, that they also may be in us, that the world may believe that you sent me."

In this prayer, Jesus is praying for unity amongst his followers. Furthermore, in verse 20 he reveals that this unity in the Christian body will affect others such that the rest of the world may believe that God sent Jesus into the world. Has there ever been a time where the world needs Jesus as it does today? If your answer is YES, then we have to stop segregating ourselves from people of other faiths and start living our lives like we are all children of the same God. That is not an easy thing to live out. As human beings we get very comfortable in living how we live. Being around people of other cultures and faiths can be extremely uncomfortable.

A simple microcosm of this is blending the practices of how we celebrate something like Christmas, when a member of our family marries someone from another culture or faith, etc. We have to learn that the relationship between people is far more important than hanging onto what you may be used to. I married a girl of Italian descent (I am of German descent). In the Italian culture my wife grew up in, Christmas Eve was celebrated with a big fish dinner followed by midnight Mass. In my family, the big celebration was a gathering of extended family on Christmas day. The big meal included kale, ham, and a German sausage made from pork mixed with an oat base. We had to learn to give and take and focus on the fact that we were celebrating the birth of our savior and not celebrating what we were used to doing.

CHAPTER 4

WE HAVE AN AWESOME GOD

I have come to realize one of the most important attitudes we must have in order to grow in our relationship with God is to see God as an awesome God. The scriptures, for some reason, refer to this awesomeness as **Fear of the Lord. Fear of the Lord** is not the state of being afraid of God from a punishment point of view. It is rather defined as being in the state of seeing God as an awesome God.

When I was telling one of my daughters about this concept of **Fear of the Lord**, she reacted by saying that it just turns her off and lessens her desire to read about it. The only thing I can tell you is that I do not have the authority to change what the Bible uses to describe this call to seeing God as awesome. So, if you find the term "**Fear of the Lord**" as a turn off, make an effort to get past that.

Psalm 138 gives us a snapshot about the magnificent ways God cares for us, his people.

¹ I thank you, Lord, with all my heart; in the presence of the angels to you I sing. ² I bow low toward your holy temple; **I praise your name for your mercy and faithfulness. For you have exalted over all your name and your promise.** *³ On the day I cried out, you answered; you strengthened my spirit. ⁴ All the kings of earth will praise you, LORD, when they hear the words of your mouth. ⁵ They will sing of the ways of the LORD: "How great is the glory of the LORD!" ⁶ The LORD is on high, but cares for the lowly and* **knows the proud from afar.** *⁷ Though I walk in the midst of dangers, you guard my life when my enemies rage. You stretch out your hand; your right hand saves me. ⁸ The LORD is with me to the end. LORD, your mercy endures forever. Never forsake the work of your hands!*

I believe the highlighted bold letters in verse 6, point out the fact that when we walk in pride we do not and cannot get as close to God as can those who are humble. God wants to know all of us on a personal level. Pride is an impediment in that relationship.

The following are a few scriptures that various prophets have said about the awesomeness of our God:

Nehemiah 1:5 *I prayed: "LORD, God of heaven,* **great and awesome God***, you preserve your covenant of mercy with those who love you and keep your commandments.*

Daniel 9:4 *I prayed to the LORD, my God, and confessed, "Ah, Lord,* **great and awesome God***, you who keep your covenant and show mercy toward those who love you and keep your commandments and your precepts!"*

Deuteronomy 10:21 *He is your praise; he is your God, who has done for you those* **great and awesome** *things that your own eyes have seen.*

Job 37:22 *From Zaphon the golden splendor comes, surrounding* **God's awesome majesty***!*

Psalm 147:5 **Great is our Lord***, vast in power, with wisdom beyond measure.*

For his audience on June 11 (I believe it was in the year 2021), Pope Francis reflected on **Fear of the Lord**: "This is the fear of God: abandonment into the goodness of Our Father who loves us so. ... This is what the Holy Spirit does in our hearts: He makes us feel like children in the arms of our Daddy ... with the wonder and joy of a child who sees himself served and loved by his Father."

Therefore, this great gift of "**Fear of the Lord**" allows us to have an intimate relationship with the Holy Trinity.

I think a perfect example of seeing our Father as awesome came out of the mouth of my grandson, Riley, when he was about four years old. We were spending weekends in our trailer in the cool country. Our daughter and Riley were visiting. My wife went for a walk with Riley when they came upon a dead bird. Riley said he would run back to the trailer to have grandpa bring his tools to fix the bird. My wife told Riley that grandpa most likely could not fix the dead bird. Riley responded by saying we needed to call his father. He would bring the right tools and fix the bird. "**My daddy can fix anything**," he said. That is seeing our daddy with awe.

This is where faith enters into the picture. The definition of faith includes the fact that we must live out our faith (see James 2:14-26). In other words, for faith to be effective we must live our lives believing that when we see God as awesome, we have the beginnings of a deeper, personal relationship with him.

Let's look at a few of the scriptures which tell us about "**Fear of the Lord**".

Psalms 111:10

*[10] The **Fear of the LORD** is the beginning of wisdom;*
prudent are all who practice it.

Proverbs 1:7

*[7] **Fear of the LORD** is the beginning of knowledge; fools despise wisdom and discipline.*

Proverbs 9:10-11

*[10] The beginning of wisdom is **Fear of the LORD**, and knowledge of the Holy One is understanding. [11] For by me your days will be multiplied and the years of your life increased.*

The wisdom and knowledge the scriptures are talking about come from the Holy Spirit. They are not worldly wisdom and worldly knowledge.

Proverbs 1:20-30

[20] Wisdom cries aloud in the street, in the open squares she raises her voice; [21] Down the crowded ways she calls out, at the city gates she utters her words: [22] "How long, you naive ones, will you love naivete, [23] How long will you turn away at my

reproof? [The arrogant delight in their arrogance, and fools hate knowledge.] Lo! I will pour out to you my spirit, I will acquaint you with my words: ²⁴ *Because I called and you refused, extended my hand and no one took notice;* ²⁵ *Because you disdained all my counsel, and my reproof you ignored* ²⁶ *I, in my turn, will laugh at your doom; will mock when terror overtakes you;* ²⁷ *When terror comes upon you like a storm, and your doom approaches like a whirlwind; when distress and anguish befall you.* ²⁸ **Then they will call me, but I will not answer; they will seek me, but will not find me,** ²⁹ *Because they hated knowledge,* **and the Fear of the LORD they did not choose.** ³⁰ *They ignored my counsel; they spurned all my reproof.*

There are many lessons in the above quoted scripture. I chose to highlight verses 28 and 29 in bold to call attention to the scriptures telling us that if we are not walking in awe of the Lord (**Fear of the Lord**) then God will not answer our prayers. In verse 29, the word tells us that **Fear of the Lord** is a decision. We choose to have **Fear of the Lord.** We choose to see God as awesome, or we don't. In actuality, we most likely do not choose **Fear of the Lord** by choosing worldly things to be attentive to.

Here are a few more scriptures regarding **Fear of the Lord** and what it produces:

Proverbs 2:1-15

*¹ **My son, if you receive my words and treasure my commands,** ² Turning your ear to wisdom, inclining your heart to understanding; ³ Yes, if you call for intelligence, and to understanding raise your voice; ⁴ If you seek her like silver, and like hidden treasures search her out, ⁵ Then will you understand the **Fear of the LORD**; the knowledge of God you will find; ⁶ **For the LORD gives wisdom, from his mouth come knowledge and understanding;** ⁷ He has success in store for the upright, is the shield of those who walk honestly, ⁸ Guarding the paths of justice, protecting the way of his faithful ones, ⁹ Then you will understand what is right and just, what is fair, every good path; ¹⁰ **For wisdom will enter your heart, knowledge will be at home in your soul,** ¹¹ Discretion will watch over you, understanding will guard you; ¹² Saving you from the way of the wicked, from those whose speech is perverse. ¹³ From those who have left the straight paths to walk in the ways of darkness, ¹⁴ Who delight in doing evil and celebrate perversity; ¹⁵ Whose ways are crooked, whose paths are devious.*

Consequently, when we walk in **Fear of the Lord**, we hook into **His wisdom and His knowledge**. When we talk about knowledge, we are talking about spiritual knowledge. Most of us are only familiar with worldly knowledge or things of the flesh).

A very clear example of operating in the spirit (as opposed to the flesh) came when a friend called one evening to ask for prayers for the adult child of a mutual friend. The adult child had been diagnosed with cancer. In our discussion, I was led to recommend reading Psalm 103 verse 3 which says, *"Who pardons all your sins, and heals all your ills."* In my mind, I was thinking that the person who was diagnosed with cancer would get hope from knowing God heals all our ills. However, what I sensed in my spirit was that God wanted me to emphasize the fact that God pardons all our sins. I did not express that part which I thought I heard in the spirit, but instead I told my friend we would pray and get back to them the next day.

Later that night, as I lay in bed, I began to pray for the person who was diagnosed with cancer. I immediately received a word of knowledge (this is in the spirit) that the root of the person's cancer was in the shame and guilt the person had from a perverted sexual experience he had been a victim of when he was very young.

I called my friend the next day to recount the word of knowledge I had received. My friend immediately responded by asking me if I had recalled a certain priest. I stopped immediately and told her that neither the priest nor any other priest had anything to do with this incident. I then told my friend that she was operating in the flesh, using the worldly knowledge she had about both parties, thus drawing what she thought was a probable conclusion. I went on to explain to her that what she just implied was an example of operating in the flesh. On the other hand, operating in the spirit is receiving knowledge about the situation from the Spirit of God. I also must say, when we receive such knowledge, it is often the case that we are not given the entire picture regarding the situation. The picture gets filled in as we continue to yield to the Spirit of God. In this particular situation, a couple of weeks later my wife and I were visiting one of our adult children. It just so happened that the location of this visit was about a thirty-minute drive to the town where my friend who had initiated the phone call lived. the person who had bee diagnosed with the cancer also lived there. Out of the blue, I heard the Spirit of God direct me to pay a visit with both of them. I was obedient and called my friend and asked her to gather the appropriate people together because I was going to be there.

I borrowed a car and drove to the town to meet those involved to explain what the specific word of knowledge meant regarding the person with the cancer. The person with the cancer immediately became defensive saying the priest never touched him. This is another example of operating in the flesh. I assured this person that it was true that no priest was involved. I went on to say that the doctors could put all the chemicals they saw fit into his body, but unless he dealt with the shame and guilt festering in his subconscious, he would not be healed.

I went on to tell this person that it would require prayer, asking God to reveal the situation of which he had no conscious memory. Everything I had just said was an example of operating in the spirit. I was, in effect, passing on to this person things that did not come from my mind (I had zero worldly knowledge about the situation), but was expressing what the Holy Spirit was telling me. We prayed over the person with no recognizable results. I was told some months later that this person was declared cancer-free. If you read that carefully you should have an example of operating in the flesh and operating in the spirit. It, in my opinion, highlights why we as Christians have to have a deep personal relationship with the Lord so He can lead us through the many stumbling blocks in our lives.

In Hosea chapter 4 and verse 6 it says:

*⁶ My people are ruined for **lack of knowledge**! Since you have rejected knowledge.*

In the New King James version, it says:

*⁶ My people are destroyed for **lack of knowledge**: because thou hast rejected knowledge.*

Let me state it again, the knowledge that is talked about here comes from the Holy Spirit. It is not knowledge we get by reading a book and telling ourselves we know God. If it is worldly knowledge, we most likely know about God but do not really know Him.

Here are a few more scriptures about "**Fear of The Lord.**"

Proverbs 10: 27

*²⁷ **Fear of the LORD** prolongs life, but the years of the wicked are cut short.*

Proverbs 14: 26-27

*²⁶ **The Fear of the LORD** is a strong defense, a refuge even for one's children. ²⁷ The **Fear of the LORD** is a fountain of life, turning one from the snares of death.*

Proverbs 15:16

*¹⁶ Better a little with **Fear of the LORD** than a great fortune with anxiety.*

Proverbs 15:33

*³³ The **Fear of the LORD** is training for wisdom, and humility goes before honors.*

Proverbs 19:23

*²³ The **Fear of the LORD** leads to life; one eats and sleeps free from any harm.*

Proverbs 22:4

*⁴ The result of humility and **Fear of the LORD** is riches, honor and life.*

Proverbs 23:7

*¹⁷ Do not let your heart envy sinners, but only those who always **Fear the LORD.***

Acts of the Apostles 9:31

*³¹ The church throughout all Judea, Galilee, and Samaria was at peace. It was being built up and walked in the **Fear of the Lord**, and with the consolation of the holy Spirit it **grew** in numbers.*

The church today is not growing in numbers. I read an article recently that stated less than half of the population in the United States attends church. I wonder if it is an indication of that "lack of **Fear of the Lord"** in many members in the church. Therefore, could this "lack of **Fear of the Lord**" be a prime contributor out of which many problems flow?

Psalms 34 verses 2-12 sum up when we have this kind of relationship with God. It begins with **"Fear of the Lord."**

² I will bless the LORD at all times; his praise shall be always in my mouth. ³ My soul will glory in the LORD; let the poor hear and be glad. ⁴ Magnify the LORD with me; and let us exalt his name together. ⁵ I sought the LORD, and he answered me, delivered me from all my fears. ⁶ Look to him and be radiant, and your faces may not blush for shame. ⁷ This poor one cried out and the LORD heard, and from all his distress he saved him. ⁸ The angel of the LORD encamps around those who fear him, and he saves them. ⁹ Taste and see that the LORD is good; blessed is the stalwart one who takes refuge in him. ¹⁰ ***Fear the LORD****, you his holy ones;* ***nothing is lacking to those who fear him.*** *¹¹ The rich grow poor and go hungry, but those who seek the LORD lack no good thing. ¹² Come, children, listen to me; I will give you* ***Fear of the LORD.***

I highly recommend the reader of this book take the time to go back over each of the above scriptures and allow them to soak into their very being. This can be done now or perhaps when one has read the entire book. Every time I read those scriptures, I am drawn deeper into just how much God loves us.

CHAPTER 5

THE SPIRIT OR THE FLESH

Growing up, I have no recollection of being taught anything about what it means to be operating in the spirit. In fact, I can honestly say I had no idea about what it means to be in the spirit. To me, the subject seemed like some abstract notion that perhaps the theologians talked about; there did not seem to be anything about it that pertained to my life. As a young boy, we went to church and I loved hearing about Jesus and the things He did when He walked on this earth. Then there was a long period where anything pertaining to God was, at best, occasionally on my mind. At those times, nothing I thought about pertaining to God invoked any kind of action on my part. When I was 26, I decided to join my wife in her faith walk by becoming baptized into the Catholic faith. I did lots of things that were considered to be spiritual such as praying with a group of men for an hour before the Blessed Sacrament (a Catholic devotion), usually on the first Friday of each month. While I am sure there was a spiritual aspect to it, I always got the sense that I did all the talking and asking but I do not remember ever hearing from God.

When I was 38, I attended a marriage retreat for the first time in my life and I heard God speak to me. When I tell people about that story they often say, that must mean you are special. That is right on the mark. I am special for several reasons. I am sure there are lots more, but let's look at three reasons why I am special. First, it tells us in the first chapter of Paul's letter to the Ephesians chapter 1:3-6:

*³ Blessed be the God and Father of our Lord Jesus Christ, who has blessed us in Christ with every spiritual blessing in the heavens, ⁴ **as he chose us in him, before the foundation of the world, to be holy and without blemish before him. In love** ⁵ he destined us for adoption to himself through Jesus Christ, in accord with the favor of his will, ⁶ for the praise of the glory of his grace that he granted us in the beloved.*

I highlighted verse 4 because it tells us that God chose me before the foundation of the world. He chose me to be holy and without blemish before

Him and he did all that with **love**. Guess what? He chose you as well and in the same way. The fact that he did this before the foundation of the world means he is talking about my spirit. This means I am a spiritual being, as are you.

In Psalms 139, the word tells us a number of things about me. Let's start with verses 13 and 14.

*^{13} **You formed my inner being; you knit me in my mother's womb.** ^{14} **I praise you, because I am wonderfully made; wonderful are your works**! My very self you know.*

God took the time to form me in my mother's womb— and he does not make mistakes.

He did that for you also.

Let's move on to verses 17 and 18.

*^{17} How precious to me are your designs, O God; how vast the sum of them! ^{18} **Were I to count them, they would outnumber the sands;** when I complete them, still you are with me.*

Wow, God has virtually endless **precious thoughts** about me! It sure looks like, in God's eyes, I am wonderful.

The same is true about you.

The three points I tried to make, and there are more, is that God knew each of us before the foundation of the world (that clearly implies we are spirit), what God creates is wonderful (actually, he does not make mistakes), and he has **endless** precious thoughts for each of us.

When God created me in my mother's womb, he evidently added the fleshy part of me. Growing up, I learned how to communicate in the flesh. I never really learned how to communicate in the spirit. In the same way that we needed to grow up and learn how to communicate in the flesh, we also need to grow up and learn how to communicate in the spirit. For most people, I propose that never happened. I will also say it is never too late.

Before we go deeper into spirit and flesh, I will try to answer the question about why God spoke to me (and my wife) on that marriage retreat. The person posing the question has never heard God speak to them. I really do not know. I don't know if God spoke solely to my wife and me, or if God spoke to all the people on the retreat, and we were just the ones who heard Him. What I do know was that I personally went on that retreat with a deep desire to love my wife and children with great passion and that I longed for a deeper relationship with God. I can tell you I jumped headfirst into what we were told on that weekend to the point where I cried trying to answer the question, "Why did you come here and what do you hope to gain?" A conclusion I have come to, as I look back to that occasion, is that I was most likely walking in **Fear of the Lord.** At the very least, I was longing for a closer relationship with God. My fleshly observation is that many, if not most people, attended such a retreat with more of a "wait and see" type of skepticism.

The following are a couple of scriptures from Matthew 16. They both involve Peter. In one case, he is operating in the spirit and in the other case he is in the flesh.

In the first scripture Peter is operating in the spirit.

*15 He said to them, "But who do you say that I am?" 16 Simon Peter said in reply, "You are the Messiah, the Son of the living God." 17 Jesus said to him in reply, "Blessed are you, Simon, son of Jonah. For **flesh and blood has not revealed this to you,** but my heavenly Father.*

In the other verses we hear the following:

*22 Then Peter took him aside and began to rebuke him, "God forbid, Lord! No such thing shall ever happen to you." 23 He turned and said to Peter, **"Get behind me, Satan! You are an obstacle***

to me. You are thinking not as God does, but as human beings do."

Here, Peter is clearly operating in the flesh.

One thing that I got from the fact that Peter walked in both the spirit and also in the flesh is that I surely do also. If he was walking with Jesus when he did that, then I am certainly subject to doing the same thing. This means to me that I must choose to walk in the spirit as much as I can. Having **Fear of the Lord**, I believe, promotes that.

I highly recommend to the reader of this book that you spend time reading and praying about Ephesians chapter 1 and Psalms chapter 1 (verses 1-3) and chapter 139.

In 1 Corinthians 2:3-5 St. Paul tells us:

*³ I came to you in weakness and fear and much trembling, ⁴ and my message and my proclamation were not with persuasive (words of) wisdom, but with a demonstration of spirit and power, ⁵ **so that your faith might rest not on human wisdom but on the power of God.***

Saint Paul goes on to say in 1 Corinthians 2:12-14:

*¹² **We have not received the spirit of the world but the Spirit that is from God,** so that we may* *understand the things freely given us by God.* **¹³ And we speak about them not with words taught by human wisdom, but with words taught by the Spirit, describing spiritual realities in spiritual terms. ¹⁴ Now the natural person does not accept what pertains to the Spirit of God, for to him it is foolishness, and he cannot understand it, because it is judged spiritually.**

Maybe the following will invoke a deep desire to learn to operate in the spirit.

In Romans 8:1-17 we read the following:

¹ Hence, **now there is no condemnation for those who are in Christ Jesus**. *² For the law of the spirit of life in Christ Jesus has freed you from the law of sin and death. ³ For what the law, weakened by the flesh, was powerless to do, this God has done: by sending his own Son in the likeness of sinful flesh and for the sake of sin, he condemned sin in the flesh, ⁴ so that the righteous decree of the law might be fulfilled in us,* **who live not according to the flesh but according to the spirit.** *⁵ For those who live according to the flesh are concerned with the things of the flesh, but those who live according to the spirit with the things of the spirit. ⁶ The concern of the flesh is death, but the concern* *of the spirit is life and peace.* ⁷ **For the concern of the flesh is hostility toward God; it does not submit to the law of God, nor can it;** ⁸ **and those who are in the flesh cannot please God.** ⁹ *But you are not in the flesh; on the contrary,* **you are in the spirit, if only the Spirit of God dwells in you. Whoever does not have the Spirit of Christ does not belong to him.** ¹⁰ *But if Christ is in you, although the body is dead because of sin, the spirit is alive because of righteousness.* ¹¹ *If the Spirit of the one who raised Jesus from the dead dwells in you, the one who raised Christ from the dead will give life to your mortal bodies also, through his Spirit that dwells in you.* ¹² *Consequently, brothers, we are not debtors to the flesh, to live according to the flesh.* ¹³ *For if you live according to the flesh, you will die, but if by the spirit you put to death the deeds of the body, you will live. Children of God through Adoption.* ¹⁴ **For those who are led by the Spirit of God are children of God.** ¹⁵ **For you did not receive a spirit of slavery to fall back into fear, but you received a spirit of adoption, through which we cry, "Abba,*̱ Father!"** ¹⁶ *The Spirit itself bears witness with our spirit that we are children of God,* ¹⁷ *and if children, then heirs, heirs of God and joint heirs with Christ, if only we suffer with him so that we may also be glorified with him.*

If you go back and read the chapter on "We Have an Awesome God" it becomes clear that when you have **Fear of the Lord** you are at the beginning of knowledge and wisdom. That is the beginning of learning to operate in the spirit and not in the flesh.

Verse 16, above, tells us that we have received a spirit of adoption and it also tells us we did not receive a spirit of fear. I can tell you this. During this time of COVID-19, I never had the slightest instance of fear. I know I am God's child so the worst thing that could happen is that I go home to my Father sooner, rather than later. That does not mean I did not take precautions, such as getting vaccinated and staying away from certain potentially harmful situations.

A number of years ago, I was filled with fear regarding a situation. I do not even remember what the situation was. In my prayer time, I asked God to take the fear from me. In my mind's eye, Jesus took me by the hand and brought me down into hell. As we walked through hell, I saw people in extreme agony and there were scary beings reaching out trying to grab me. Jesus said to me, **"Stay close to me and nothing can harm you."** He then said, "I want you to taste the love of my Father, the same love that raised me out of this place." I became enveloped in a great and very comforting love and the earth opened and I found myself back in my room praying. If I ever get tempted to have fear, I remember that experience and focus on staying close to Jesus.

Finally, Saint Paul tells us in his letter to the Galatians, chapter 5; 1,13-26 the following:

1 For freedom Christ set us free; so stand firm and do not submit again to the yoke of slavery.

13 For you were called for freedom, brothers. **But do not use this freedom as an opportunity for the flesh; rather, serve* one another through love. 14 For the whole law is fulfilled in one statement, namely, "You shall love your neighbor as yourself."*** *15 But if you go on biting and devouring one another, beware that you are not consumed by one another.* **16ᴵ I say, then: live by the Spirit and you will certainly not gratify the desire of the flesh.* 17 For the flesh has desires against the Spirit, and the Spirit against the flesh; these are opposed to each other, so that you may not do what you want. 18 But if you are guided by the Spirit, you are not under the law.** *19 Now the works of the flesh are obvious: immorality, impurity, licentiousness, 20 idolatry, sorcery, hatreds, rivalry, jealousy, outbursts of fury, acts* *of selfishness, dissensions, factions, 21 occasions of envy,* drinking bouts, orgies, and the like. I warn you, as I warned you before, that those who do such things will not inherit the kingdom of God.* **22 In contrast, the fruit of the Spirit is love, joy, peace, patience, kindness, generosity, faithfulness, 23 gentleness, self-control. Against such there is no law. 24 Now those who belong to Christ [Jesus] have crucified their flesh with its passions and desires. 25 If we live in the Spirit, let us also follow the Spirit.** *26 Let us not be conceited, provoking one another, envious of one another.*

CHAPTER 6

WHAT IS FAITH?

Let's begin our discussion about the definition of faith with a couple of scriptures.

Hebrews 11:1-6 tells us:

*¹ **Faith is the realization of what is hoped for and evidence of things not seen**. ² Because of it the ancients were well attested. ³ By faith we understand that the universe was **ordered by the word of God,** so that what is visible came into being through the invisible. ⁴ By faith Abel offered to God a sacrifice greater than Cain's. Through this he was attested to be righteous, God bearing witness to his gifts, and through this, though dead, he still speaks. ⁵ By faith Enoch was taken up so that he should not see death, and "he was found no more because God had taken him." Before he was taken up, he was attested to have pleased God. ⁶*

But without faith it is impossible to please him, for anyone who approaches God must believe that he exists and that he rewards those who seek him.

James 2:14-26 tells us:

¹⁴ What good is it, my brothers, if someone says he has faith but does not have work? Can that faith save him? ¹⁵ If a brother or sister has nothing to wear and has no food for the day, ¹⁶ and one of you says to them, "Go in peace, keep warm, and eat well," but you do not give them the necessities of the body, what good is it? ¹⁷ **So also faith in itself, if it does not have works, is dead.** *¹⁸ Indeed someone may say, "You have faith and I have work." Demonstrate your faith to me without works, and I will demonstrate my faith to you from my works. ¹⁹* **You believe that God is one. You do well. Even the demons believe that and tremble.** *²⁰ Do you want proof, you ignoramus, that faith without works is useless? ²¹ Was not Abraham our father justified by works when he offered his son Isaac upon the altar? ²²* **You see that faith was active along with his works, and faith was completed by the works.** *²³ Thus the scripture was fulfilled that says, "Abraham believed God, and it was credited to him as righteousness," and he was called "the friend of God." ²⁴ See how a* *person is justified by works and not by faith alone. ²⁵ And in the same way, was not Rahab the harlot also justified by works when she welcomed the messengers and sent them out by a different route?* **²⁶ For just as a body without a spirit is dead, so also faith without works is dead.**

I need to clarify what is meant by "works" in this area. Faith is not something we say we believe but never apply it to our lives. The simplest example I can think of is applying faith by living what it says in the following scriptures. Let's start with 1 Thessalonians 5:16-18:

¹⁶ Rejoice always. ¹⁷ Pray without ceasing. ¹⁸ In all circumstances give thanks, for this is the will of God for you in Christ Jesus.

This means whether something happens to me that I think is good or if something happens that I think is bad, I give thanks to God. Why? Because it is God's will for me (and for you). When I tie this scripture to Romans 8:28 I know God will turn all things together for good because I am doing His will.

Romans 8:28 says:

²⁸ We know that all things work together for good for those who love God, *who are called according to his purpose.*

What it means to love God is defined in 1 John 5:3.

³ *For the love of God is this, that we keep his commandments.* *And his commandments are not burdensome.*

I live out my faith by giving thanks to God for all things, because that is His will for me and because I know He will turn all things together for good. I may not always see the good and that is why I walk in faith knowing that good things will come out of it. Why will good come out of it? Because God said it would in His word as expressed in Romans 8:48, cited above. It's that simple.

Let's look at the subject of tithing. I selected this subject for several reasons. First, for the purpose of explaining about faith, it is fairly clear. There is nothing ambiguous about it. Secondly, it will get most people's attention, either in a positive way or it will hit home regarding the level of faith we have.

In the book of Haggai, chapter 2 verse 8, God tells us all the silver and all the gold is mine.

⁸ *Mine is the silver and mine the gold* —*oracle of the LORD of hosts.*

When we realize all the silver and all the gold is His, and we know all money is backed by silver or gold, then the following makes sense with regard to robbing God, in part, because God owns all the money. Let me repeat that in another way. If all money systems are backed by silver and/or gold, and if God owns all the silver and gold, then He owns all the money. He wants the money He has given to you to be used to touch the lives of others.

In the book of Malachi chapter 3 verses 7-10 we are told:

7 Since the days of your ancestors you have turned aside from my statutes and have not kept them. Return to me, that I may return to you, says the LORD of hosts. But you say, "Why should we return?" **8 Can anyone rob God? But you are robbing me! And you say, "How have we robbed you?" Of tithes and contributions!** *9 You are indeed **accursed**, for you, the whole nation, rob me. 10 Bring the whole tithe into the storehouse, that there may be food in my house.* **Put me to the test, says the LORD of hosts, and see if I do not open the floodgates of heaven for you, and pour down upon you blessing without measure!**

A tithe is defined as 10%. God is saying when you get money (which is already His), you should take the first 10% of that money and pass it on to others. He is saying two major things. One is if you chose to not tithe, then you are robbing Him, because He is asking you to give the first 10% of what He gave you to someone in need. Another way to put it is that He is trusting you to give a portion of His money, which He just gave to you, to someone else. Failure to do so is breaking the deal He gave you, which in His eyes is stealing from Him.

The second part of the deal is that when you do what He asks (and this is one place in the scriptures where He asks you to try Him in this) then He will pour out heaven's blessing upon you. The action of giving the tithe is **walking in faith**.

Allow me to tell you how we came to the decision to tithe and what resulted when we did so.

At the time, we still had one of our children in attendance at the University of Arizona and our son was attending the local Jesuit High School. I was looking forward to his moving on to college because the tuition at the state university was significantly less than the tuition at the Jesuit High School. In addition, I was hoping I could put aside enough money to be able to take an early retirement.

While attending a Charismatic Convention in Los Angeles, my wife and I both heard, in our spirit, to send Christopher to Loyola Marymount University (LMU), a Jesuit institute located in Los Angeles.

In addition to that we also heard, in our spirit, that God was calling us to begin to tithe. Now that is not "something that seems right to a man." Remember Proverbs 12:14 and 16:25 cited in Chapter 3, above. There was one more caveat added to the whole equation, which made it even more bizarre (from a fleshly point of view) being the fact that Anita had been recruited to leave her job in the public schools in order to teach Spanish in the Jesuit High School. If she took that job, it would mean she would be taking a pay cut.

I told God we needed to run this by our girls as they all attended the University of Arizona (U of A). Deep inside, I was hoping they would give me reasons why Christopher should go to the same school they attended. Quite the opposite occurred. They not only encouraged us to send him to the Jesuit University, but they each offered to help with the expenses if we could not afford it. There went that excuse. As an aside, the girls, at times, gave Christopher some spending money, saying a boy needed more money to date than a girl might need.

In my prayer time, I told God we would send Christopher to LMU and that we would begin to tithe, but the tuition had to be considered as part of the tithe. I was quite sure God accepted that. Anita also accepted the job at the Jesuit High School.

We paid the tuition for both Christopher at LMU and Cathy at the University of Arizona in August of that year. When we paid the same tuition for the second semester, we depleted all that we had saved for our children's college education. Furthermore, our combined incomes were such that we would not be able to keep up with the tuition at LMU the following summer.

Over the Christmas holidays, my wife received a phone call from the mother of two students she had in one of her classes who were from Mexico. They were attending the Jesuit High School to learn English. The mother asked Anita if we would be willing to house both boys while they continued to study here in the USA. My wife and I discussed it and said why not! I mean, "What does it take to feed a couple of more kids?"

When the family arrived with the boys in January, the mother pulled Anita aside and gave her some money to pay for the room and board. We did not expect that. It turns out the money we received made up for the money we needed to send Christopher to LMU. The one boy graduated that spring and the other boy brought his cousin with him for the following year. I received some generous raises during this period and by the time they left, we were able to finish paying for Christopher's stay at LMU.

God's generosity and His favor will not be outdone. I have only told you part of the story. We were blessed far beyond the material side of the story. Oh, and yes, when we had paid the last semester's tuition for LMU, we heard in our spirit that God wanted the rest of the tithe. We complied and have been extremely blessed ever since.

Let me call your attention again to verse 9 from the scripture quoted above:

⁹ *You are indeed **accursed**, for you, the whole nation, rob me.*

What the spirit of God is telling us is that we are accursed when we don't bring in the whole tithe.

In our marriage, there were times when we had tensions between us as husband and wife, and even within me, as I worried about how we would afford things. I can only tell you that in our case, when we began tithing, all the tensions we had regarding money went away. I believe those tensions were a spiritual problem.

I want to share with you one more story regarding having faith in God's word. In Matthew 18:20 it says:

²⁰ *For where two or three are gathered together in my name, **there am I in the midst of them**."*

A few years ago, I had a lot of pain in my lower back. My doctor suggested a series of three shots in the spine to relieve or eliminate the pain. In those days that procedure was performed in the hospital. I went into the hospital the evening before the procedure and I had been told I would be given a shot of Demerol prior to starting the series of shots. When I awakened the next morning, I asked God to send a nurse who was a believer so that I would be assured that at least two of us believed, and then I would know He was present. About 20 minutes later, the nurse walked in to administer the Demerol. When she walked into my room, I said to her "You must be a believer." She responded saying that she was indeed a believer, so I asked her to pray with me that the entire procedure would go well.

We prayed and then she administered the Demerol. I commented that I had not seen her at the nurse's station. She told me she was from another floor and that someone had called down to her station to have someone come and give me my shot as they were very busy at the moment. Coincidence? I think not. My doctor came into my room sometime after the first shot and said he did not understand why, but I was free to go home as the first shot did the job.

I will close with the following scripture from 1 Thessalonians 2:13:

¹³ And for this reason we too give thanks to God unceasingly, that, in receiving the word of God from hearing us, you received not a human word but, as it truly is, **the word of God, which is now at work in you who believe.**

Note one must believe the Word of God for it to take root in us and one must exercise the works it was intended to perform. This means we must apply the Word of God to our lives for it to be effective.

CHAPTER 7

HEARING GOD SPEAK

It has not been unusual for people to ask me, "How do you hear God?" or "How do you know it is God speaking to you?" Another thing people have said to me is, "Well you are special." We talked about that in Chapter 5 and how we were all created by God, etc. What some people mean by that is that God favors me. Quite frankly that is analogous to saying that mom or dad loved you more than he or she loved me. Since Psalm 139 tells us that God's precious thoughts for each of us outnumber the sands, we can put that notion to bed right now. God's love has no favorites.

I can tell you right up front that I cannot create a complete list of how to hear God. My hope is that what I share is helpful to you in this area.

The following scripture might be useful:

John 10:25-29

*25 Jesus answered them, "**I told you and you do not believe**. The works I do in my Father's name testify to me. 26 **But you do not believe, because you are not among my sheep.** 27 **My sheep hear my voice; I know them, and they follow me.** 28 I give them eternal life, and they shall never perish. No one can take them out of my hand. 29 My Father, who has given them to me, is greater than all, and no one can take them out of the Father's hand.*

It sounds like we need to be a believer in order to hear God. I'll say it again: being a believer means one lives out what God is calling us to do in His Word. Sheep are, by nature, followers of their Shepherd. Going to church does not necessarily make one a follower of Christ. If you are a follower of Christ, then you yearn to live as he calls one to live. That is more than being nice to people (The Golden Rule). Let's look at a couple of things the Word tells us about that:

In John 8:42-43, Jesus tells us the following:

42 Jesus said to them, "If God were your Father, you would love me, for I came from God and am here;

I did not come on my own, but he sent me. ⁴³ **Why do you not understand what I am saying? Because you cannot bear to hear my words.**

Those are pretty strong words. Let's keep going. In John 14:15-17 Jesus is talking to his disciples.

¹⁵ **"If you love me, you will keep my commandments.** ¹⁶ *And I will ask the Father,* **and he will give you another Advocate to be with you always,** ¹⁷ **the Spirit of truth,** *which the world cannot accept, because it neither sees nor knows it. But you know it, because it remains with you, and will be in you.*

Here, He is talking about receiving the Holy Spirit. At another time the disciples ask him about doing God's work. Here is what Jesus said, as stated in John 6:28-29.

²⁸ *So they said to him, "What can we do to accomplish the works of God?"* ²⁹ *Jesus answered and said to them,* **"This is the work of God**, *that you* **believe** *in the one he sent."*

Believe, there is that faith thing again. I was playing golf with a pastor friend of mine and he told me that he did not know if he believed in healing. I asked him, "Then whose work are you doing?" I mean, after all, Jesus was a healer and He told us to do the same.

Let's take a look at what Jesus said to the disciples and to the whole Church for that matter.

In Matthew 10:5-10 Jesus is telling his disciples to heal the sick.

⁵ *Jesus sent out these twelve after instructing them thus, "Do not go into pagan territory or enter a Samaritan town.* ⁶ *Go rather to the lost sheep of the house of Israel.* ⁷ *As you go,* **make this proclamation: 'The kingdom of heaven is at hand.'** ⁸ ***Cure the sick, raise the dead, cleanse lepers, drive out demons.*** *Without cost you have received; without cost you are to give.*

In Luke 10:8-9 Jesus is talking to those who are following His disciples.

⁸ *Whatever town you enter and they welcome you, eat what is set before you,* ⁹ ***cure the sick in it and say to them, 'The kingdom of God is at hand for you.'***

So, one of the things Jesus asks us to do is to heal the sick. He also asks us to proclaim the presence of the Kingdom of God. This is just the beginning of the list of things He wants us to do. In order to do this, the scriptures above – Matthew 10:5-10 and Luke 10:8-9 – tell us we will need the Holy Spirit.

In the last century, healing burst forth amongst some Christian churches in the early 1900's when there was a new outpouring of the Holy Spirit. I was at a charismatic conference listening to a talk given by a priest who said the Pope at the time had asked the bishops around the world to pray on New Year's Eve for a new Pentecost. He said a man in Topeka, KS was deeply touched by the Holy Spirit the very next day. The spirit then moved to what is known as the Azusa Street Revival. It reached the Catholic church in 1967 when a group of people were on a retreat at Duquesne University in Pittsburgh, Pa.

What am I getting at? I think there are three main things that are needed to begin to hear the voice of God. One is **Fear of the Lord**. When one has **Fear of the Lord, one is at the beginning of both knowledge and of wisdom**. These are spiritual knowledge and wisdom. The **second is the Holy Spirit**. I will talk about the baptism of the Holy Spirit in another chapter. The third item is **faith,** which we talked about earlier.

When Jesus stood before Pontius Pilate, the following exchange took place, as told from John 18:37-38.

37 *So Pilate said to him, "Then you are a king?" Jesus answered, "You say I am a king. For this I was*

born and for this I came into the world, to testify to the truth. **Everyone who belongs to the truth listens to my voice."**

³⁸ *Pilate said to him, "What is truth?"*

If you do not hear the voice of God then maybe you live by "a truth" that does not line up with Jesus. Let's see what the word of God says about the truth.

1 Kings 17:24

²⁴ *The woman said to Elijah, "Now indeed **I know that you are a man of God, and it is truly the word of the LORD that you speak."***

From the New King James Bible, the wording is as follows:

²⁴ *Then the woman said to Elijah, "Now by this **I know that you are a man of God, and that the word of the Lord is in your mouth is the truth."***

John 14:6

¹⁴ *Jesus said to him, "**I am the way and the truth and the life.** No one comes to the Father except through me.*

When trying to listen to God, the first thing is one cannot put God in a box. What I mean by that is that God can use whatever means He chooses to get our attention. So rather than look at God, let's look at our own behaviors and attitudes. The onus, I believe, is on us to put ourselves in a position to hear God.

In the book of Genesis chapter 1 verse 27 we are told:

²⁷ God created mankind in his image; in the image of God he created them; male and female he created them.

One of the aspects of that is that if we are created in His image, then we should be able to communicate with our maker. Communicate means speaking and hearing.

One question that we need to wrestle with is, "Who is in charge of my life?"

For most of us the answer is fairly clear. I am in charge of my life. (And yes, we are, as God gave each of us free will). After all, we have been taught and trained to take responsibility for our actions. And this is good. But God tells us in Mark 10:15 that we must become like a little child or we cannot enter into the Kingdom of God. This means we must learn to be childlike whereby we become dependent upon God, just like a child is dependent upon his or her parents. That is sort of in conflict with how we were raised to be self-sufficient. I found that I had to change my inner thinking to knowing I cannot do certain things without direction from God. What helped me do this was when I got into the healing ministry, I would ask God to have the next person who came for healing be the same as the last person I prayed with. In that way, I would know how to proceed. It never happened. When I know how to proceed, then I am in charge. I quickly learned I needed to get my thinking out of the way and move into a state of needing God, if anything good was going to occur. How do I do this? I admit to myself that I do not have a clue as to what to do and I invoke faith that God will provide the direction I need. It means, in some cases, that I am willing to look like a fool.

I also tend to lean toward praying in tongues to help me to get out of the equation. (Praying in tongues? We need an in-filling of the Holy Spirit to do that. Thus, the Baptism of the Holy Spirit). I switch back to English when I get a thought while praying in tongues that directs me to do so. I believe this is hearing God. In any case, I find that I must slow down and just listen, rather than do all the talking. I'll talk about the gifts of the Holy Spirit and why I think we need to be baptized in the Holy Spirit in Chapter 9.

Let me interject right here that the notion of **Fear of the Lord** also comes into play when we want to hear from God. Remember, in Chapter 4, we talked about **Fear of the Lord**. **Fear of the Lord** is the beginning of both knowledge and wisdom. The knowledge and wisdom we are talking about comes from God. It is not worldly knowledge and wisdom. When God talks to us, He is giving us both spiritual knowledge and spiritual wisdom.

One of the things we need to consider is whether or not we have expectations of God talking to us in a certain manner. In the book of 1 Kings, we find the prophet Elijah running from those who want to kill him. He ends up hiding in a cave in the mountains. We pick up the story in 1 Kings 19:11-13.

¹¹ Then the LORD said: Go out and stand on the mountain before the LORD; the LORD will pass by. There was a strong and violent wind rending the mountains and crushing rocks before the LORD—but the LORD was not in the wind; after the wind, an earthquake—but the LORD was not in the earthquake; ¹² after the earthquake, fire—but the LORD was not in the fire; after the fire, ***a light silent sound.*** *¹³ When he heard this, Elijah hid his face in his cloak and went out and stood at the entrance of the cave. A voice said to him, why are you here, Elijah?*

So, the question we have to ask ourselves is, do we expect God to talk to us in some spectacular way or do we quiet down and hear Him in a whisper?

Another behavior that I believe prevents us from hearing God lies in how we pray. Let me explain. I find that when I am with a person that "talks non-stop" I get the sense that when I do get a chance to give my input, my input is not heard by the non-stop talker.

When we equate that to prayer, the question is how do you pray? Do you do all the talking? If you do all the talking, how do you hear from someone? If someone is doing all the talking, he or she may hear words coming from someone else, but the act of talking focuses on what they themselves are saying in order to have something to say. When my wife and I were in leadership in the Marriage Encounter movement, I would often ask someone who was dealing with a problem whether or not they prayed about their particular situation and, many times, the answer was, "Yes I did pray and God did not do what I told him I needed."

Quite frankly, it is my opinion that that kind of prayer is on the arrogant side. Simply, prayer can't be "me" based. Scripture tells us that we enter the gates through praise. When you think about it, the person is telling God what to do. Wow! The chances are that you already know the answer to such a prayer. The answer never comes. Not only that, but God already knows what is needed. The question that should be asked of God is "what should I do?"

Once we see God as awesome (we have **Fear of the Lord**), we can begin to hear God. Perhaps we can compare it to going to a foreign country. If we are not open to learning the language spoken there then we will never really understand what people are saying. Perhaps we can tie it to the fact that we as little children learned to speak, hear and understand by immersing ourselves into being with parents, family, etc. We learn to hear something that makes sense by practice.

I have found that in order to hear God, my prayer time must include lots of listening rather than talking. Furthermore, I find I need to get out from any emotions that might be controlling my thoughts and my behavior. How do I do that? I like to answer questions with a lived example. I often will ask God for a scripture that might apply to what I am trying to discern.

A number of years ago we were trying to sell our house at a time when houses just were not selling. We were blessed to have a buyer. We had also committed to the purchase of a new home. We would be in a terrible bind if the sale of our house did not go through. One day, in the middle of all this, the buyer of our house asked to allow him to inspect our air conditioning system. It was over 20 years old. The buyer was in the air conditioning business. I allowed my imagination to lead me into thinking the worst, namely that the buyer would change his mind after inspecting the air conditioner. That alone put me in an emotional state by which it would be difficult to listen. The fear of not being able to close on the house convinced me that I had a problem.

In my prayer time I asked God to give me a scripture that would ease my fears. Much to my surprise, I heard Exodus 7:20 which tells us about Moses striking the river with his staff and the river turning to blood (this was in reference to Moses requesting that his people be set free from the Egyptian ruler). I asked God, "What does this have to do with selling my house?" I heard in my spirit, "If I can change the river into blood, I can certainly sell your house." I decided God was in charge and all my fears left me. Sure enough, the sale of the house went through.

When I was 57, I got a job offer to start working for a small privately-owned company. I had trouble settling down in my prayer time to listen to God about taking this job. My wife came home one day and said she was attending Mass at the school where she worked and she asked God what we should do about my taking the job offer. She said what came to mind was a fictional story about a flood whereby the authorities came to the man and told him he should evacuate. He told them God would rescue him. The flood waters rose so high that the man had to climb up onto his roof. A rescue boat came along asking the man to jump on board. The man said he would stay where he was because God was going to rescue him. The flood waters got even higher and the man was perched atop of his chimney when a helicopter came by to rescue him. The man declined, stating God was going to rescue him. He eventually got swept away by the flood water and drowned. When he got to heaven, he asked God what happened, why didn't he keep His word and save him. God said, "I sent the authorities in a truck, but you declined. Then I sent a life boat and you declined again. Finally, I sent a helicopter and you chose to not climb aboard."

My wife said she thought this job was my life boat. I took the job and it was the best job I ever had. I retired from that company some 20 years later.

Here's another example of how God has responded to my requests for help. I was at church one Sunday and my upper back was filled with pain. I did not know where I should go for help. I asked God to lead me to the right doctor. When we were leaving church, there was a crowd of people all going out through the door at the same time. I looked at the crowd and everyone in the crowd seemed to be a blur except for a friend of mine who happened to be a physician in another area of medicine. When I got out of the church, I approached my friend to see if he could recommend a doctor for my problem. He directed me to another doctor from our church. I called his office and made an appointment. In a couple of visits, he got my pain to disappear and told me it was likely caused by my computer being too low for my line of sight. I went to work and asked management to raise the height of my desk and the pain never came back. Notice, in this case God did not speak to me directly, but rather pointed out who I should go to.

I have found that God often puts thoughts in my mind when I am not even asking. Let me give you an example. When my wife and I were approaching our 50th wedding anniversary, we decided rather than have a party, we would celebrate with a family affair by having our four children and their spouses along with their children spend a week with us at the beach in San Diego. We chose that because for most of the years when our children were still at home, we spent one or two weeks each summer staying in a campground near the beaches.

During those years we all stayed in a tent trailer that slept eight people. When the children became teenagers, we often had some of their friends with us as well. Sometimes we had so many people that some slept outside on cots. In any case, we had a lot of fond memories.

Consequently, for our 50th anniversary we decided to rent two beach houses that were right on the beach. During the weeks that preceded this event I began to sense that I was to send one of our married children some money to help with their families' expenses. I hesitated doing this because I was actually being self-righteous with regards to how I thought they were not handling their money the way I would. The sad part is I never talked to them about it, I just came to that conclusion on my own. Consequently, I did not send them any money, even though I was pretty sure those thoughts I had about sending money came from God. Then, one evening, while we were having dinner a neighbor stopped by just to chat. I don't know why, but I mentioned to this neighbor what I had been wrestling with in regards to sending our daughter and her family some money. My neighbor responded by telling me how she had lost her own daughter to drugs and tearfully suggested I send the money, which I did.

When our daughter and her family arrived for the festivities, she took me aside and told me that if we had not sent the money, they would not have been able to attend. When I looked back, I realized God was "planting" the thoughts to send the money and, after it had all passed, He told me He had sent the neighbor over in an attempt to break through my being self-righteous. I have a number of stories of God prompting me to give to others, but you should get the idea that sometimes we get promptings from God. It is up to us to recognize them and to act on them. One thing I have learned is to recognize a prompting when it comes by the simple fact it is a thought that comes to me about something I am not even thinking about. I have also found that when I don't respond it is because of being self-righteous or I have unhealed pain in my subconscious that controls my willingness to do things, like help others.

CHAPTER 8

MISSING GOD'S COMMAND

I believe it is important to not only be familiar with the scriptures but also to incorporate the scriptures in our lives. Allow me to talk about a time when I was not sure that God was talking to me. During a Forgiveness and Healing workshop we were presenting, a married couple approached us and asked for prayers because they had been unable to conceive a child. While we were praying over them (laying on of hands), a thought popped into my head to tell them they needed, among other things, to be grateful. At that point in our walk with God I can say I had become familiar with 1 Thessalonians 5:16-18 but had not started to incorporate it into my life. Consequently, I did not pass that on to the couple.

1 Thessalonians 5:16-18 is about rejoicing always regardless of the situation.

When we finished praying over the couple, we went on with the workshop. We had no idea what the outcome was for the couple. Since we were holding the workshop out of town, we never had any follow-up with the couple.

However, there was follow-up with the Holy Spirit. When we went to bed that evening, I began to sense the Holy Spirit was not happy with me. I cannot tell you how that felt except the subject kept coming into my mind that I had failed to encourage the couple to rejoice. We flew home from the city where we held the workshop but the same sense of the Holy Spirit did not leave me. Monday morning, while in the shower, getting ready to go to work, I finally asked the Holy Spirit for forgiveness and said I would try not to let that happen again. Immediately, I sensed the Holy Spirit wanted me to contact my best friend who had just been laid off from his job on the day we were leaving to give our workshop. The Holy Spirit intimated that I should tell my friend that he and his wife needed to be obedient to God's word by being grateful and by praising God (this reveals that we trust in Him more than our circumstance). I told God I would be obedient and pass that message on to him and his wife.

A little background is in order. My best friend and his wife had six children; his wife stayed home to care for their children. I had heard about the layoff on Friday when I left work, but did not have time to contact them to talk about what happened.

When my coffee break time came, I called their house and my friend answered the phone. We talked about what had happened with his being laid off, and all sorts of things related to it. I then told my friend that the Holy Spirit had a message for them: they were to rejoice and thank God for the situation they were in. My friend called his wife and told her the call was for her. It was a comedic reaction to what I had just laid on him. She got on the phone as well as he, and I referenced the scripture from 1 Thessalonians explaining what it meant and why. I told them I had a book called "Power in Praise" by Merlin R. Carothers, which I suggested they read. I happened to have my copy of the book at work, so at noon I delivered it to their house. They started to read it immediately and were so touched by its message they ran out to the bookstore to get a second copy. They both wanted to read it and had trouble putting it down.

They were in a leadership role in the Marriage Encounter Movement which put them in a position where many people in the diocese knew them. They began praising God openly and lots of wonderful things happened. Members of the movement started dropping things off to help their financial situation. My friend was so moved by the Holy Spirit that if he saw someone with a financial need and he had money in his pocket, he would give the person in need what he had. I started to become nervous thinking maybe he was going off the deep end. Wrong!

We had one of our Forgiveness and Healing Workshops scheduled at the local parish and we invited them to experience the workshop. While having lunch together during the workshop, my friend told me that during the prayer to forgive, he prayed for and forgave the man who had laid him off. I responded by telling him he needed to contact the man who laid him off to ask for forgiveness for the anger my friend had for the man. I have to tell you I don't know where my response came from, so I must have been prompted by the Holy Spirit to say such a thing.

The following Thursday my friend called me to ask for prayers as he was going to meet with the man who laid him off. My reaction was to ask what prompted him to do that. He said, "I had told him he needed to do it."

Their meeting was scheduled for early Thursday afternoon. While sitting at my desk eating my lunch I began to pray for my friend and the meeting that was about to take place. Suddenly, I got a very strong urge to head for the men's room. While walking down the hall, one of the software development managers stopped me to ask if I knew someone with certain software credentials as he himself had a high priority assignment and needed help in a certain area. He wanted to hire someone ASAP. I told him I had a friend who was immediately available (I did not mention the layoff status) whose work experience might fill the bill for him. The manager asked how quickly I could contact my friend to see if he was interested in the job. I told him I could have my friend there in an hour or two. The manager was thrilled and said he would stay by his phone awaiting the call.

The funny thing happened was that my urge to go to the men's room had left me.

I went downstairs to the area where my friend was meeting with the man who had laid him off. The office door was closed, so I asked one of the employees if he knew why the door was closed. He told me that my friend, who had been laid off, was in the office. I thanked him and boldly walked over to the closed door and stuck my head in. It was not well received, but I asked the manager to call me when they were finished as I had to talk to my friend and that I would take responsibility to escort him out of the building.

I brought my friend up to the manager who was looking to hire someone ASAP. During the interview, the manager decided my friend did not have the qualifications he needed but the manager in the next office also had a need for a new employee. Since that manager was not at work that day, he had two people from the other manager's team interview my friend. They were favorably impressed. The next day the other manager called my friend in for an interview and was also favorably impressed. It also turned out that my friend had worked with this manager's brother when they both worked for a Wall Street firm in NYC. When the manager called his brother over the weekend, his brother told him my friend was one of the hardest working, competent employees with whom he had ever been associated.

When the manager went to hire my friend, he discovered the previous manager had written "Not for Rehire" in my friend's personnel file.

The hiring manager took his brother's assessment of my friend and had to work his way all the way up to a vice president to get the "Not for Rehire" expunged from my friend's personnel file. He got the job.

Some people might say that was a bunch of coincidences; I see it as the Holy Spirit working in our lives.

CHAPTER 9

DISCERNING GOD'S WILL

Many of us were taught that if we went to church every Sunday (and in the Catholic Church, that included Christmas and other designated Holy Days) and if we followed certain other rules designated by the church that we were doing God's will. The goal of all of this kind of behavior was to make it into heaven. I have no intention of discussing the pluses and minuses of what I just stated, but rather I hope to show that God wants a personal relationship with each and every one of us. That being said, it follows that God's will for us, in many cases, is to direct our lives in a way that we would experience the peace, joy and love that He wants for us. So, why would He want that for us? Well, let's look at Genesis 1 verse 27:

*²⁷ God created mankind in his image; in the image of God, he created them; male and female*He created them.*

We can also look at Psalms 139 verses 13-14.

¹³ You formed my inner being; you knit me in my mother's womb. ¹⁴ I praise you, because I am wonderfully made; wonderful are your works!

In 2 Timothy 3 verses 16-17, the word tells us that the scriptures are of God and they give us the ability to do good work.

***¹⁶ All scripture is inspired by God** and is useful for teaching, for refutation, for correction, and for training in righteousness, ¹⁷ **so that one who belongs to God may be competent, equipped for every good work**.*

We are God's creation. He is our Father and each of us is His child. What parent does not want what is best for their child? Furthermore, God knows what each of us needs to live a happier, and more peaceful life, which includes being loved and loving others. In addition, He prepares us through the scriptures to perform His work. I have learned through experience that there is nothing more joyful than to know you were led by God to perform His work.

I would like to share with you a few things I learned about discerning God's will for me (and us as a married couple).

Let me start with an experience we had on a retreat for married couples, called Marriage Encounter. Some friends had asked us to go on this retreat because they had gone to such a retreat and said they couldn't even describe what it had done for them. They took us to a meeting at one of the Catholic churches where another couple gave a motivational and informative presentation about the retreat. There were quite a few people at that meeting, about half of whom had experienced the retreat. We thought why not, as we had never been on a retreat for married couples; we signed up. We did not realize this retreat was offered weekend after weekend, not only in the city where we lived, but all over the U.S. and in other countries as well.

The retreat consisted of a series of talks with the subject of each talk pertaining to the marriage relationship. In the case of the Catholic version of the retreat, each talk was given by a married couple and a priest. There were three couples as part of the retreat team. We found out later that this same retreat was given in other churches.

I am quite sure the team there consisted of three couples and a minister, or a married minister and his wife. In any case, my wife and I found ourselves deeply touched by each talk that was presented during the retreat. After each talk, we were given a question or two to answer and then we were to exchange our answers with our spouses, discussing what each of us had written. We separated, husband and wife, while we wrote; I assume so as to not be a distraction to one another. On Saturday afternoon of our retreat, as I was finishing my answers to the questions we had been given, I heard, deep in my spirit, God telling me He wanted me to change my life.

People have asked, "did you hear something audible?" The answer is no. It was deep in my spirit, kind of like a thought had been planted, yet I knew it was from God. When the writing time ended, we were excused to go back to our rooms where our spouses were writing their answers to the same question(s). I can only tell you I was overwhelmed because I had never heard God speak to me before this. When I got to the room, my wife opened the door as I was putting the key in the lock and excitedly told me she had something to tell me. I told her to go first even though I was bursting to tell her what I had experienced. She said she had heard God tell her He wanted us to change our lives. We just held each other and cried.

I have to say that the intent of the weekend was to get married couples and priests who attended the weekend to change their lives. The call, simply stated, was to get the couples and priests to love more deeply and to carry that love out to the rest of the world.

I am sad because, here too, oftentimes when we tell our story people will conclude that we must be special. That is true. We are special. In fact, we are all special in God's eyes. I'll hit that subject later in the book. I am also saddened that so many people came away thinking that the weekend retreat made them feel high and they wanted to stay that way.

When we tell our story about this experience people often ask, "How do you know it was God?" I can only say you know because you know. We did not know what "change our lives" meant but when the retreat was over, we were presented with opportunities to touch the lives of other people.

The first such example was when we were asked by the presenting teams to consider joining them for future weekend retreats. Actually, we were asked to consider attending a second retreat designed to have us look even deeper into our marriage and to discern if we were called to that ministry. We also discussed the whole thing with our four children and they encouraged us to follow the path we were on. We left the second weekend with no doubt that entering into this ministry was God's will for us.

During that second weekend, during our prayer time, I promised God I would read the entire Bible. I remembered that my Lutheran Pastor had told me that if you read one chapter each day and three chapters on Sunday, that you would read the entire Bible in about a year.

I have to tell you that I do not read very well. I do not remember reading even one book in high school. I made up books in order to satisfy my English teacher's requirement for outside reading. My mother worked in the pediatrics department at the local hospital and the clinical psychologist associated with that department offered to test my reading skills. The test revealed that I read very slowly, and my retention was poor. He suggested classes for remedial readers. We could not afford to pay for such classes so I never went. The college I attended recommended the same thing at the end of my freshman year. Again, I could not afford it, so I lived with the results that came from not being able to read well. I also had trouble memorizing. Years later, my wife figured out that I am probably dyslexic.

All that being said, I finished reading the entire Bible in about a year. The only exception was the book of Revelation. I fell asleep every night trying to read it, so after some time I dropped the idea. There were passages in the Bible that clearly gave me directions for my life. I would highlight them with a colored marker so that I could find them again. When I got done, I had quite a few highlighted scriptures but in most cases I could only remember, at best, the general area of the Bible where they were.

One evening at a meeting, another married couple approached us asking where in the Bible they could find some direction about obtaining wisdom about something they were dealing with. I told them I would pray about it and get back to them. In actuality, I had no idea where this might be discussed in the Bible. Our oldest daughter said she was quite sure there was an appendix in her version of the Bible that listed scriptures pertaining to key subjects in the Bible. I looked in her Bible and found a reference to a scripture pertaining to seeking wisdom. I read the scripture and then called the couple to do the same. That scripture is in the book of James, chapter 1 verses 5-8.

*5 **But if any of you lacks wisdom, he should ask God who gives to all generously and ungrudgingly, and he will be given it.** 6 But he should ask in faith, not doubting, for the one who doubts is like a wave of the sea that is driven and tossed about by the wind. 7 For that person must* *not suppose that he will receive anything from the Lord, ⁸ since he is a man of two minds, unstable in all his ways.*

I have given that same scripture to many people since then and I certainly refer to it in my own life often.

What I discovered was that many people have never heard God speak to them. At least they might not have recognized the voice of God. Consequently, suggesting that one should ask for wisdom made no sense if you cannot discern God's answer.

When I look back at the whole scenario of the couple asking us for guidance on how to discern and then my having to research it to give them an answer, I realize it may just have been God's way of getting me to move into the power that exists in His Word.

Let me give you an example of an instance that highlighted what a lack of faith might look like.

A couple of years ago we decided to move into a Retirement Resort Community whereby we would no longer have to maintain a house, etc. In order to make that move, among other things, we had to sell our house. Since we were in our late seventies, we were not as sure about what steps to take to do this. One morning at breakfast it came up in our conversation that it was a little confusing as to what we should do and when we should do it.

I suggested we ask God to give us wisdom, as it states in the book of James, quoted above. My wife, who is very organized and persistent, made that request each day that followed. After the third or fourth day of asking for wisdom, and not hearing anything, I suggested that just maybe asking over and over again was a sign of lack of faith. If you ask, God will answer, so why are we asking over and over? "Then how should we pray?" she asked. My response was that since God's Word promised He would give us the wisdom we asked for, then we should begin praising and thanking Him for the wisdom He was about to give us. So, we did just that. Each morning we thanked Him for what wisdom we received and for what we were about to receive. I can only tell you it seemed like God was holding our hands in leading us through the steps we needed to take. That even included placing our dog in a very loving home.

Now one warning, because we as humans are always looking for a formula to follow. When we know the formula, then we don't need God's wisdom— or so we think. Trusting God step by step does several things for us. The first is that we will receive the best advice we can possibly get.

The second is that as we walk in faith, we grow closer to God and we realize more deeply that He is our Father who takes care of us.

Father Chuck Gallagher, S.J., a priest who was a driving force behind the Marriage Encounter movement gave us a couple of what I will call high-level adages to help discern if something is God's will for you.

The first is, "If everyone is doing it, it is probably not Gospel." By "everyone" he meant if many people are doing it. At least that is the way I interpreted what he was saying. For example, many couples are choosing to live together before marriage. That is most likely not Gospel. The list could go on forever. Living together before marriage would be a red flag (something to look at) as far as living the Gospel goes.

The second adage is "If it is reasonable, it is probably not Gospel." When my wife and I would present this adage during a workshop, or even when just talking about the subject with someone, it was not unusual for the person or persons to push back in disagreement. Go back and read Proverbs 14:12 and/or Proverbs 16:25. It says:

There is a way that seems right to a man (that makes it reasonable in that person's way of thinking), *but its end is the way to death.* (New King James Version (NKJV)).

The scriptures are filled with passages that clearly and simply state what God's will is for each of us. Let me list just a few of them. Some are less reasonable than others.

1 Thessalonians 5:16-18

16 Rejoice always. *17* Pray without ceasing. *18* In all circumstances give thanks, for this is the will of God for you in Christ Jesus.

Most people that I have come in contact with are fairly intelligent and quite capable, so a way that seems correct to them has to be reasonable, and therefore the way to proceed.

While we can argue that giving thanks for all that is happening to us is not reasonable, it is more reasonable, at least to me, than the following:

Luke 6:30

30 Give to everyone who asks of you, and from the one who takes what is yours do not demand it back.

I have to admit I find it much harder to live out what verse 30, above, is saying. It is, for me, much more unreasonable to give to all who ask, than it is to give thanks as 1 Thessalonians 5:18 calls us to do. I mean, let's face it, giving thanks, even if we would rather not do so, doesn't really cost us anything. Whereas giving to all who ask might mean departing with some money.

Let me give you a couple other scriptures to think about that are clearly God's will for each of us.

Matthew 5:22-24

²² But I say to you, whoever is angry with his brother will be liable to judgment, and whoever says to his brother, 'Raqa,' will be answerable to the Sanhedrin, and whoever says, 'You fool,' will be liable to fiery Gehenna. ²³ Therefore, if you bring your gift to the altar, **and there recall that your brother has anything against you, ²⁴ leave your gift there at the altar, go first and be reconciled with your brother,** *and then come and offer your gift.*

The reasonable thing to do in the case stated above is to hang onto my anger and either wait for or demand the other person to make amends before I let it go.

I cannot tell you how many people have disagreements in their families and they stand on some principle like, "He started it, so he needs to come to me and ask forgiveness," or "I am the father of this family, so it is up to my child to come to me and ask for forgiveness." How does that kind of thinking fit under the basic call of the Christian to "love your neighbor as you love yourself?"

Matthew 5:3-5

³ Why do you notice the splinter in your brother's eye, but do not perceive the wooden beam in your own eye? ⁴ How can you say to your brother, 'Let me remove that splinter from your eye,' while the wooden beam is in your eye? ⁵ You hypocrite, remove the wooden beam from your eye first; then you will see clearly to remove the splinter from your brother's eye.

Simply stated, **God is telling us to look at our own faults rather than stand on being right in your own mind.** That is just not reasonable. But it is clearly God's will for each of us.

Another suggestion we were given to help us discern God's will for us is to consult with the best Christians you know. What I discovered with going down this path is that I needed to very carefully discern what the person I go to is saying. If the person you go to for help has the answer without asking for clarification regarding the situation, you might just be dealing with a "know it all." In case you have never heard the term, "know it all," it generally means the person has a huge ego and probably does not have the wisdom you are seeking.

I think a fair example of this occurred when my wife received papers from her uncle to sign. The papers to sign were required to satisfy the distribution of her grandparents' estate. This estate was from her father's side of the family and she was included because her father was deceased. Rather than sign the papers, my wife chose to consult with a friend as to what she should do. He gave her advice, solely based on legal implication, to ask her uncle for more information.

I don't remember the friend asking any questions about the situation. She did what the friend suggested and it backfired in that her uncle was insulted that she did not trust him. On top of that, the dollar amount she was to receive was quite small. The papers he sent to her supported what he had told her in the first place. The problem was the uncle cut off relations for a long time. Up to that point, her uncle had been sending generous gifts to our family at Christmas time. That ended. I know that many of the readers of this example will hold on to the fact that he should have sent the supporting documentation in the first place. From a worldly point of view, that is correct. From a family relationship point of view, it backfired and, in my opinion, was just not worth it. The point I am trying to illustrate is that discerning some things requires more discernment when the person you go to never asks a thing about the entire situation.

CHAPTER 10

BAPTISM OF THE HOLY SPIRIT.

The first baptism of the Holy Spirit came at the Jordan River right after Jesus had asked John the Baptist to baptize Him with water.

Mark 1:7-11 tells us the following:

*7 And this is what he proclaimed: "One mightier than I is coming after me. I am not worthy to stoop and loosen the thongs of his sandals. 8 **I have baptized you with water; he will baptize you with the holy Spirit.** " 9 It happened in those days that Jesus came from Nazareth of Galilee and was baptized in the Jordan by John. 10 On coming up out of the water he saw the heavens being torn open **and the Spirit, like a dove, descending upon him.** 11 And a voice came from the heavens, "You are my beloved Son; with you I am well pleased."*

I find it interesting that Jesus was baptized with water by John the Baptist and then He was baptized with the Holy Spirit. Verse 8, above, clearly shows the separation of the two baptisms. I wonder why a number of churches have eliminated the second part, namely the baptism of the Holy Spirit.

The first baptism of the Holy Spirit for the rest of us came at Pentecost. **Prior to Pentecost, Jesus told His disciples to not begin any ministry until they had received power from God.**

In Luke 24:49, the apostles were told to not begin their ministry until they received the Holy Spirit.

⁴⁹ And [behold] I am sending the promise of my Father upon you; ***but stay*** *in the city* ***until you are clothed with power from on high."***

Saint Paul tells us that the kingdom of God is lived out on the spiritual level, not in the flesh.

Romans 14:17

*¹⁷ For **the kingdom of God** is not a matter of food and drink, **but of righteousness, peace, and joy in the holy Spirit;***

He also tells us that the kingdom of God is about power. When He says it is not about talk, He is telling us one cannot persuade one's self (or anyone else) into the kingdom of God by giving a good speech (or a sales pitch).

1 Corinthians 4:20

*²⁰ **For the kingdom of God is not a matter of talk but of power.***

1 Corinthians 15:50

Here, He makes it clear one cannot enter into the kingdom of God while operating in the flesh. One must be in the spirit to enter into God's power.

50 This I declare, brothers: ***flesh and blood cannot inherit the kingdom of God,*** *nor does corruption inherit incorruption.*

Entering into the Kingdom of God is a spiritual thing. After all, we are both spirit and flesh. The Scripture in Romans 6:11 tells us that we have been crucified with Christ and that we are to reckon yourselves dead. We need to drop the flesh part of us and operate in the spirit. I cannot tell you how many people go totally silent when I start talking about things pertaining to operating in the spirit. Their eyes kind of gloss over like we are in two different worlds. If a person is not born again (baptized in the Holy Spirit), we are in two different worlds (realms).

In the Acts of the Apostles, chapter 19:1-6, it talks about two different baptisms:

¹ While Apollos was in Corinth, Paul traveled through the interior of the country and came (down) to Ephesus where he found some disciples. ² He said to them, "Did you receive the Holy Spirit when you became believers?" They answered him, "We have never even heard that there is a Holy Spirit." ³ He said, "How were you baptized?" They replied, "With the baptism of John." ⁴ Paul then said, "John baptized with a baptism of repentance, telling the people to believe in the one who was to come after him, that is, in Jesus." ⁵ When they heard this, they were baptized in the name of the Lord Jesus. ⁶ And when Paul laid [his] hands on them, the Holy Spirit came upon them, and they spoke in tongues and prophesied.

The Gospel of John, chapter 3:1-7, talks about being born again:

¹ Now there was a Pharisee named Nicodemus, a ruler of the Jews. ² He came to Jesus at night and said to him, "Rabbi, we know that you are a teacher who has come from God, for no one can do these signs that you are doing unless God is with him". ³ Jesus answered and said to him, **"Amen, amen, I say to you, no one can see the kingdom** *of God without being born from above." * *4* *Nicodemus said to him, "How can a person once grown old be born again? Surely, he cannot reenter his mother's womb and be born again, can he?" 5 Jesus answered, "Amen, amen,* **I say to you, no one can enter the kingdom of God without being born of water and Spirit** *6* **What is born of flesh is flesh and what is born of spirit is spirit.** *7 Do not be amazed that I told you,* **'You must be born from above.'**

1 Peter 1:23-25

23 You have been born again through the living and abiding word of God which does not perish. **You have been born anew**, *not from perishable but from imperishable seed,* **through the living and abiding word of God,** *24 for: "All flesh is like grass, and all its glory like the flower of the field; the grass withers, and the flower wilts;* 25 **but the word of the Lord remains forever." This is the word that has been proclaimed to you.**

In the Acts of the Apostles, there are many recordings of the power of God manifesting in such things as healing and deliverance from evil spirits by the apostles and the early church. This all occurred after Pentecost when the power of the Holy Spirit fell on them.

CHAPTER 11

WHERE DID THE POWER GO?

In his book, *"The Nearly Perfect Crime,"* Francis MacNutt tells us that in the first several hundred years of the church, every believer was healed. The power to heal was very prevalent. He goes on to say that about that time, the church fathers decided to eliminate the specific practice of Baptizing in the Holy Spirit and they also introduced infant baptism. If I understand it correctly, the church at that time indicated that the Holy Spirit entered into the picture via the water baptism and via the Sacrament of Confirmation.

MacNutt goes on to say that the evidence of healing also left the church. He said in some cases certain orders of priests/brothers took on the notion that they were not "Holy enough" to be practicing praying for healing so they stopped the practice altogether.

Francis MacNutt is the author of many books with regards to healing. Perhaps his most famous book was entitled, "Healing." Many people refer to that book as the most complete book on that subject. I am told that the book was his bestseller with over 400,000 copies sold. MacNutt had been an ordained Catholic priest who left the priesthood and opted to be married.

He and his wife have a healing ministry that is known worldwide. He was reconciled with the Catholic Church and is a practicing Catholic. I mention this because I have been told by some people that since he chose to leave the priesthood one should not associate with him and his ministry. I can only guess that those who profess that either do not know he has reconciled with the church or perhaps they don't believe in reconciliation.

My wife and I attended a number of Southern California Renewal Ministry Conventions over the years. At one such convention, we listened to a priest present a paper on the History of the Charismatic Renewal in the Catholic church. In that presentation, we were told that the Pope at the turn of the century (1899-1900) asked the bishops throughout the world to pray for a new Pentecost.

The presenter went on to say that on January 1 (which was the next day), a man in Topeka, KS was overcome by the power of the Holy Spirit. The man was of another faith. Shortly after that, the power of the Holy Spirit broke out in a church called Azusa Street in Los Angeles. If you wish to know more about it, look up Azusa Street on the internet.

What happened at Azusa Street was a huge break out of the power of the Holy Spirit. In fact, people of many faiths were also seeking the power of the Holy spirit in their lives. Note there is documentation regarding the power of God being exercised in the early 1900's and, in fact, prior to that in the 1800's. Two such men that I have read about are John G. Lake and Smith Wigglesworth. The healing and miracles that are chronicled regarding these men are well worth investigating.

Also notice, here were the Catholic Bishops praying for a new Pentecost and lo and behold the new Pentecost first appeared to people of other faiths. Our God is amazing. I wonder what He had in mind. Getting back to what occurred in the early 1900's— needless to say, this break out of God's power received very mixed reviews. Isn't that part of human nature? Some Christians were overwhelmed by the manifestation of God's power, whereas others rejected what was happening and went so far as to call it demonic. Oh, how mankind does not take to new things happening very easily! It is not surprising, when you think about it. When Jesus walked the earth and was casting out demons, the unbelievers said it must come from the prince of demons. In Matthew 12:24, the religious of that day said the following:

²⁴* But when the Pharisees heard this, they said, "This man drives out demons only by the power of Beelzebul, the prince of demons."

In 1967, a group of Catholic people were attending a retreat at Duquesne University when the Power of the Holy Spirit fell upon the attendees. This was the beginning of what is called the "Charismatic Renewal." The power of the Holy Spirit quickly exploded through the entire church worldwide. However, just like at Azusa Street, there were many people who rejected it. What happened with those who accepted and welcomed this power from the Holy Spirit was an explosion of healing and other manifestations of God's power.

Unfortunately, large enough segments of the church (and not just the Catholic Church) still choose not to incorporate this power into their everyday life.

A few years ago, a popular movie called, "Jerry Maguire," hit the big screens. The movie was about a sports agent (Jerry Maguire) played by Tom Cruise. The sports figure he was trying to sign was a football player, Rod Tidwell, played by Cuba Gooding Jr. A famous line from the movie was when Rod Tidwell told Jerry Maguire if he wanted to sign him, he needed to "show him the money." What does that have to do with the subject of this chapter?

Well, if eliminating the Baptism of the Holy Spirit has no effect on the life of the church, **then show me the manifestation of the power of the Holy Spirit throughout the whole church.** Particularly in light of John 14:12.

*[12]{} Amen, amen, I say to you, whoever believes in me will do the works that I do, and **will do greater ones than these**, because I am going to the Father.*

It, in general, does not exist. When I read the Acts of the Apostles, I am confronted by two things: The apostles went about preaching the Word and they baptized their people in the water and in the Holy Spirit. The church grew in numbers and was alive in God's power. Can we say that today?

I have to tell you my experience of being baptized in the Holy Spirit and the effects it had on my spirituality.

Before I get to that, a little background is in order. I have mentioned several times that my wife and I had a powerful experience on the Marriage

Encounter weekend. Our spirituality continued to deepen as we involved ourselves in that ministry. Several years after we made the weekend and while we were in a leadership role within the Marriage Encounter Movement, I ended up in the hospital with clinical depression. During my stay in the hospital, and in the months that followed, I began reading a plethora of books pertaining to the subject of healing and deliverance. These books were a byproduct of the new Pentecost that I talked about, above. The books I read were from authors of different Christian faiths. I was so moved by what I read, that I decided God was going to heal me and I started attending sessions where people with the gifts of the Holy Spirit (healing, discernment of spirits, etc.) were speaking.

In one of my trips to the religious book store, the store owner invited me to attend a "Life in the Spirit Seminar," which ended in being prayed over for the baptism of the Holy Spirit. I declined because I judged I already had God in my life. When she told me one of the sessions would include a "Healing of Memories" she got my attention.

I attended the seminar but did not really participate with much effort. When they prayed over me for the baptism of the Holy Spirit, I did not receive anything

I could identify as a deeper walk with God. I mean, after all, I already had a deep relationship with Him. How is that for an attitude?

About a year after we started to give workshops on Forgiveness and Healing, the Diocesan Director of the Charismatic Renewal asked us to give the workshop on Forgiveness and Healing for the prayer group leaders for the Diocese. During that workshop, the Holy Spirit directed me to ask forgiveness for my attitude toward needing Baptism in the Holy Spirit. The next day I was praying in tongues and most of the other charismatic gifts followed including healing, discernment of spirits, and words of knowledge. I have prophesied a number of times. I believe I witnessed three miracles of healing and I had the gift of interpretation of tongues one time. My desire to read the scriptures increased fairly dramatically. It has been my observation that hunger for the scriptures is very present in most people who became baptized in the Holy Spirit.

I cannot even begin to count the number of people who were healed or delivered from evil spirits over the years. A number of people told me they were dying in the hospital and were healed when I prayed with them. These are people of all faiths. The same is true about receiving words of knowledge.

I cannot count the number of people who have been touched when the word of knowledge was present. Seeing God as an awesome God (Fear of the Lord) combined with being baptized in the Holy Spirit are what opens us up to God's power, God's wisdom and God's knowledge.

CHAPTER 12

CONFRONTING EVIL

I spent a long time debating with myself as to whether or not to include a chapter about the existence of evil. I finally decided it is foolish to ignore the subject, pretending it does not exist. I also decided it is unfair to people to not let them know that evil spirits can affect our behavior and can be the source of sickness.

That being said, the contents of this chapter will not discuss any "how to" with regard to removing or chasing away the spirits. There are plenty of books regarding this very subject. One such book that I read recently is called "Unbound" by Neal Lozano. Here, too, one should be walking in a very close relationship with the Lord before even considering entering into the battle with evil spirits. The intention of this subject in this chapter is to make the reader aware of the problem and to give the reader a few varied examples with regards to the subject.

What I will talk about in this chapter is not only the fact that evil spirits exist but they can wreak havoc with the lives of people. I will do this by documenting my own experience in various situations. By the way, what I will describe in the chapter about "We Have Two Angels" is not an evil spirit. In that case, I am talking about the spirit of someone who died and was afraid to move on after the body had died.

In the sixth chapter of Ephesians, the writer tells us our struggles are with evil spirits.

*10 Finally, **draw your strength from the Lord and from his mighty power.** 11 Put on the armor of God so that you may be able to stand firm against the tactics of the devil. 12 For our **struggle is not with flesh and blood but with the principalities, with the powers, with the world rulers of this present darkness, with the evil spirits in the heavens.***

I cannot even begin to know how one can deal with evil spirits unless they have received God's power by being baptized in the Holy Spirit.

I have had people say to me that this notion of evil spirits was how they looked at things way back in time. They say modern psychology has the real answer to our woes. That kind of thinking is clearly operating in the flesh. Remember in Matthew 16 verses 22-23 Jesus told Peter, when he suggested Jesus not go up to Jerusalem, that he was operating in the flesh with that statement and Jesus actually called what Peter was suggesting as satanic.

Just a few words about what Saint Paul is telling us in Ephesians 6. First, we must draw our strength from the Lord and His mighty power. In order to draw our strength from the Lord and from His mighty power, we must enter into the kingdom of God. This means that first we must become children of God by knowing Christ as our savior and by walking in Fear of the Lord.

Secondly, we must be baptized in the Holy Spirit. It means we must be operating in the spirit and not in the flesh. In order to utilize God's power, we must operate with God's wisdom and His knowledge.

Furthermore, we are kidding ourselves if we think we can operate by denying the existence of evil. So many people seem to take a stand that says, "I don't want to think about evil spirits and so I will pretend they don't exist."

I do not remember how I got into the ministry of delivering Christians from evil spirits. It just seemed to happen when I would be praying over someone who was either sick or having relationship problems.

I ended up discipling under the tutelage of someone who was a very prayerful and holy person. I often consulted with this person and was given advice and direction. The person also gave me audio tapes which taught and advised me about the subject. I called this person once or twice a week to relate what I had experienced with regard to confronting evil spirits and to ask for advice, particularly when I was not sure how to handle a particular situation.

At one point I was seeing so many people with spiritual problems (evil spirits) that I asked if I could possibly be putting too much focus on this very subject. The person assured me that I was not doing that, but stated that God would send people to anyone He trusted to help deliver the person from the offending spirits. Over time, the person revealed to me that she had actually been an aid to the priest who had been the diocesan exorcist.

Let me state right now that not all situations require exorcism as defined by the Catholic Church. If you saw the movie "The Exorcist," get that out of your mind right now. That movie was a Hollywood presentation which, in my opinion, was not even close to the reality that I was seeing. That is all I will say about it.

Both 1 Peter chapter 5, and Ephesians chapter 4 give reference to the devil. In 1 Peter 5:25-26 it says:

²⁵ Therefore, putting away falsehood, **speak the truth***, each one to his neighbor, for we are members of one another. ²⁶ Be angry but do not sin;* **do not let the sun set on your anger,** *²⁷* **and do not leave room for the devil.**

The truth we are talking about is Godly truth, not worldly truth. In order to receive and understand Godly truth, one must be operating in the spirit, not in the flesh. Peter goes on to tell us that staying angry opens one up to the wiles of the devil.

In Ephesians 4:6-9, we are told:

⁶ So humble yourselves under the mighty hand of God, that he may exalt you in due time. ⁷ Cast all your worries upon him because he cares for you. ⁸ Be sober and vigilant. **Your opponent the devil is prowling around like a roaring lion looking for [someone] to devour. ⁹ Resist him, steadfast in faith, knowing that your fellow believers throughout the world undergo the same sufferings.**

In both scriptures, the author is talking about how a Christian should behave and then references the devil. I have seen cases where repeated instances of living out behavior that is contrary to how God is calling us to live seems to leave the door wide open for the devil to get a foothold with that person. Here again, one does not discern the presence of a devil with someone based on what is said here. That would be operating in the flesh by drawing such a conclusion. The spiritual world has to be dealt with when operating in the spirit.

Let's look into John 10:10, which tells us:

¹⁰ *A thief comes only to steal and slaughter and destroy; I came so that they might have life and have it more abundantly.*

Notice, Jesus is talking about the existence of demons when he refers to the thief.

I will only say this at this time. Things like sickness, in my mind, do not come under the notion of abundant life. I have had people tell me that sickness is God's will for you. Really? Keep that in mind– I will get back to that a little later.

One of my earlier confrontations with the evil one came when a priest friend of mine asked if my wife and I would talk to a man from his parish who, at times, would become very angry and, during the times of anger, would inflict physical harm on his loved ones. He would then be very repentant, at least until the next time.

The man visited with my wife and me for counseling and prayer. When praying over him, no anger issues manifested. It just so happened we were doing a healing workshop at a parish across town the following Saturday. At my suggestion, the man and his wife came to the workshop. The man's wife indicated she was at her wits end. He did not seem to get anything from the workshop. So, I am sure she went home quite disappointed.

The following Monday, while on lunch break, I was praying for him when I received a word of knowledge. I called my priest friend to tell him the man would explode into another rage within the next two days. The priest called the man's wife and she confirmed what I had received in the word of knowledge. The priest set up a team of people to pray over him for that evening. The team consisted of the priest, three prayerful women from a nearby parish, plus my wife and me. I took the lead and it was not long before spirits manifested and the man rose out of the chair threatening harm to all of us. I looked over and one of the women was praying in the spirit (also known as tongues). Her eyes were closed and she was in total peace. This spurred me to command the person we were praying over to sit down.

I then told the man to declare "Jesus as Lord." With much difficulty he finally got the words out of his mouth and his demeanor immediately returned to a person who was also at peace. To my knowledge, he has never had another experience of rage again. It turns out he had apparently been beaten quite often by an angry father when he was growing up.

It is human nature to see something or read about something and then try to emulate that very behavior in an attempt to get the same results. For example, one might think that if they are praying for someone who is dealing with evil spirits, then it's best to just tell the person to say the words, "Jesus is Lord," just like in the example I've described. That would most likely be operating in the flesh. In the above example, when I told the person to proclaim Jesus as Lord, I was most likely operating in the spirit when those words came out of my mouth. In other words, one has to be led by the Holy Spirit whenever one is praying for healing or praying to deliver a person from evil.

The next story I would like to share with you occurred in another city where we were doing our healing workshop. Right after our praying for people to recognize and forgive people in their lives who in some way had hurt them, we asked the people in attendance to form small groups and share what they had experienced, if they were willing to do so. An ordained priest who had come to the workshop approached me and asked if he could share with me and the priest that was part of our team. My wife joined another sharing group.

The priest began by stating he was terrorized by a nun at his parish and it was affecting him greatly. I asked him when was the first time he ever experienced terror. He said when he was very young and was molested by an uncle. I asked him if he ever experienced terror at other times in his life. He had been brought up in a war-torn country and said that whenever soldiers from the occupying nation came around, he would hide under the porch in complete terror.

To that I said, "Let's pray." During the prayer I bound the spirit of terror and commanded it to leave and not come back. He belched, and when questioned, he said he saw a black ball leave his mouth and travel upward. His entire demeanor became very relaxed. Thirty or more years later, our daughter learned from a friend that he had been at a reunion with the graduates from their class in the seminary. During the reunion, a priest told the story of how he had gone to a workshop on forgiveness and how he had been delivered from the spirit of terror. He went on to say that being delivered from that spirit had totally changed his life and his priesthood. Praise God.

A married couple came to see my wife and me for healing prayers. She had a number of miscarriages over a period of time. She went to the doctor who told her she had a condition by which she would never be able to carry a baby full term. When we were praying over her, I got the sense she was dealing with a lot of fear. When I asked her about it, she indicated that was indeed true and, in general, she dealt with fear on a regular basis ever since her childhood.

I said, let's pray some more. While praying I quietly bound up the spirit of fear and told it to leave and never come back. When she got home that evening, she called to ask me if I had done some sort of delivery from fear while I was praying. She said she was asking because she had been burping all the way home, which was something she never did. I told her I had told the fear to leave and asked if she was OK with that. She said she was as she had some knowledge of the subject from discussions with a relative who attended prayer meetings. She and her husband had two more children after that deliverance and to her knowledge never had another miscarriage. Do they all go that easy? Of course not. Sometimes it gets messy. I have no plans to go any further into the subject of deliverance. I mentioned one book at the beginning of this chapter. There are lots of books regarding the subject.

My wife, at one time, had been unfairly treated by a couple of fellow workers. The situation was ignored by management. I won't go into details but I will say what had occurred was against labor laws. The problem persisted for over a year. I was conflicted. Part of me wanted to file a lawsuit. At the same time, I didn't really believe in suing.

One night, my wife was experiencing an asthma attack, something she rarely had. Her medicines did not seem to bring her any relief so I sat on the bedside and prayed over her while gently massaging her back. I prayed for over an hour before she fell into a restful sleep. The problem was that I was now wide awake and could not get to sleep. Consequently, I decided to go downstairs and read the Bible and pray quietly, hoping the experience would make me sleepy.

While praying and reading the Bible, the word **vindictive** kept coming to my mind. I even got the Bible dictionary to see if any of the words I was reading were related to vindictiveness. I knew they were not, but I was now disturbed by what I was experiencing. I finally stopped and asked God to show me what was occurring. He began to show me instances pretty much through my entire life where, in my heart, I wanted to get even for what had happened to me. I realized I had a vindictive heart even though I never tried to get even, except perhaps when my brother and I fought.

I finally started to cry and I shouted to God that I no longer wanted to carry this vindictiveness. Suddenly I stopped and commanded the spirit of vindictiveness to leave me and never come back. I can only tell you I felt this mass leave my chest, come up and stretch my throat, and then stretch my mouth even more so. This thing left me and I became filled with joy and peace like I never remember having. I sat there and praised God until about 5:00 A.M. and then went to bed and slept soundly.

At that time in my life, I was riding my bike to work each day along the irrigation canals that run through Phoenix. I could sense a group of evil spirits trying to attack me. This kind of thing could be really scary to some people. I just kept announcing aloud that Jesus was my Lord and Savior. They finally left me alone after a week or so.

In Matthew 12:43-45 the word of God tells us the following:

*⁴³ "When an unclean spirit goes out of a person it roams through arid regions searching for rest but finds none. ⁴⁴ Then it says, 'I will return to my home from which I came.' But upon returning, **it finds it empty, swept clean**, and put in order. ⁴⁵ Then it goes and brings back with itself seven other spirits more evil than itself, and they move in and dwell there; and the last condition of that person is worse than the first. Thus, it will be with this evil generation."*

Luke 11:24-26 tells us the very same thing:

In verse 44 of Matthew 12, cited above, the scripture talks about the person **being empty and swept clean.** I am told this is referring to a person who does not have a strong relationship with the Holy Spirit. That leaves them vulnerable to even more evil spirits. In each of the examples I shared above, the people involved had a strong relationship with God.

In this example, since it involved me, I want to point out that repeated anti-gospel behavior over time opens up the door to the devil. In this case, I never acted on my desire to be vindictive (or get even) when someone offended me in some way. I just allowed vindictiveness to remain in my heart. I am sure the presence of that spirit of vindictiveness had affected my peace and joy and it even played a part in the depression I went through. In addition to that, I am also sure that by carrying this vindictiveness around in my heart I either kept people at arms-length because I did not trust them, or I shied away from helping others because I had not healed the hurt that led to my vindictiveness.

One more story about confronting evil spirits. In the Gospel of Mark 5:6-10 is the story of a band (for lack of a better word) of evil spirits.

*⁶ Catching sight of Jesus from a distance, he ran up and prostrated himself before him, ⁷ crying out in a loud voice, "What have you to do with me, Jesus, Son of the Most High God? I assure you by God, do not torment me!" ⁸ **(He had been saying to him, "Unclean spirit, come out of the man!")** ⁹ **He asked him, "What is your name?" He replied, "Legion is my name. There are many of us."** ¹⁰ And he pleaded earnestly with him not to drive them away from that territory.*

It is also chronicled in Luke 8:30.

Jesus had confronted a man that had many spirits and dealt with them. We had a similar experience.

We had a person come to our home for prayer. I won't go into any detail about what the person told us. Shortly after we began to pray, this person went to the floor and began to growl like an enraged animal. I immediately sensed hundreds of evil spirits surrounding us. For a very short instance I received a glimpse of them. It was, to say the least, a very unnerving experience. My wife, who never swears, looked at me and said to get that person out of here. It took about a half hour to get the person back to a normal countenance. I asked the person for permission to put a team together to try to free the person from these spirits.

I am skipping a lot of details, but we realized the spirits were called **legion.** We could not find anyone to join us in dealing with the situation and probably the worst part was that the spirits would not leave our house. Whenever anyone came into the house, they were gripped with evil. Some people sensed it and others did not. I tried everything I knew to get them to leave but to no avail. Coincidentally, a priest friend of ours had offered to celebrate mass in our home (our home was very new) as part of blessing our home. I did not want to alarm him, so we chose to not tell him what we had been dealing with. When we celebrated the mass, the spirits left our home and never came back. Praise God!

Most people we have had contact with want nothing to do with the whole notion of evil spirits. Some do not believe they exist, some become skittish or afraid of the subject, some equate it to a movie they have seen. It is kind of like thinking if I ignore reality, it will go away. I have seen people do the same thing with things like cancer.

They have the symptoms, but somehow their behavior is to ignore the symptoms and I am guessing in their minds they think it will go away. This kind of thinking is very strong and is often a destructive form of denying reality. Denying reality can have very strong consequences.

I had an interesting experience when an evil spirit talked to me through a person I had been praying with.

I had prayed over this person a number of times. Then, one day, as I approached the person in public with no intention of any interaction, I heard in my spirit, with a very sarcastic expression, "Oh, it's you again." I was taken aback for several reasons. The person did not speak to me. Our eyes just met. There was no audible sound, yet my spirit heard it very clearly with a sarcastic expression that told me, "You have been a pain in the butt to me."

Another way to express the sarcastic tone is, "Go away, you have been really annoying." When I walked on by, there was a manifestation of the evil spirit in the person's persona, which made me realize it was the evil spirit that had communicated with me. I stopped and prayed in tongues and the manifestation disappeared.

I consulted with a priest friend that I know had dealt in the arena of evil spirits. He agreed it was the presence of an evil spirit (or spirits) and offered to help deliver the person from them. When I contacted the person and their close family members, I related to them about what I had experienced. I suggested they pray about the situation and perhaps consult with their pastor to see if they wanted to deal with the situation. I never heard from them, so I assumed they did not want to deal with it.

Let's get back to John 10:10.

10 A thief comes only to steal and slaughter and destroy; I (Jesus) came so that they might have life and have it more abundantly.

The evil one is very cunning. He will use whatever he can to destroy God's people. That being said, sickness does not come from God. Sickness is not a bearer of abundant life. In the example I gave of self-delivering a spirit of vindictiveness, the spirit apparently entered by virtue of the fact that I carried vindictiveness in my heart for many years. I believe the same is true for things like anger, hate, deception, bitterness, etc. In any case, when one harbors such things, it leaves one wide open to the destructive nature of the evil spirits.

So, what do we do about it? Get rid of your anger, and let go of things like hatred, resentment and bitterness. Stop deceiving people. Repent of one's sinful behavior.

One time I had a counseling session with a very holy woman who had the gift of discernment regarding one's walk with God. She told me I had a spirit of rejection but that God did not want her to deliver me from it. He instructed her to tell me I needed to love myself and when I loved myself the spirit of rejection would leave on its own. Well, I learned to love myself and the spirit apparently left quietly. See the chapter on "The Truth Will Set You Free."

Having learned to love myself, I no longer am bothered by a sense of rejection.

I need to say just a few words about pornography. I have not personally researched the subject but I do know it is far more serious and far more prevalent than most people realize. I am told something like 86% of men are addicted to pornography, including ordained ministers and priests!

I cannot even tell you when pornography begins.

A person I know passed along a story of what had happened in his life. Like many men, he enjoyed seeing beautiful women. He said he never acted on what he viewed other than to just look. He said he noticed when he got on the internet and there was an article about how some movie star looked in her new bikini, he took a look at the article. One day he realized articles like these were showing up on his computer with higher frequency. Then he noticed that articles showed up that advertised dating sites with beautiful women. Over time they became more explicit.

Still, he thought what the heck, everyone must experience this. And, of course, he never talked about it with anyone, nor did anyone broach the subject with him. He was jolted with a real awakening when he went into a store to purchase something and an attractive woman came out of the office to wait on him. He said he suddenly had the urge to grab the woman and do whatever. He realized that this urge came from "an outside force." He told it to leave him alone. After that incident, he stopped looking at the articles that displayed attractive women in their swimwear. He then realized that over time the frequency of the articles became less and less. What is the message here? Such behavior becomes habitual and eventually leads to a state of addiction. That is NOT from God. I am told that, like any addiction, getting set free from it is not easy. Most people face their addictions from a psychological perspective. I have no doubt that this one would most likely require some spiritual deliverance as well.

CHAPTER 13

WHEN I AM WEAK IS WHEN I AM STRONG

In Saint Paul's second letter to the Corinthians, Saint Paul is talking about a thorn in his side. In 2 Corinthians 12:8-10 it says:

⁸ Three times I begged the Lord about this, that it might leave me, ⁹ but he said to me, **"My grace is sufficient for you, for my power is made perfect in weakness."** *I will rather boast most gladly of my weaknesses,* **in order that the power of Christ may dwell with me.** *¹⁰ Therefore, I am content with weaknesses, insults, hardships, persecutions, and constraints, for the sake of Christ; for when I am weak, then I am strong.*

I have to say it took me a long time to even consider delving into this subject. I think it was drilled into me when I was growing up to stand up and be strong. Consequently, I lived most of my life thinking I needed to know the answers to whatever I faced. One of the behavior patterns that came out of that kind of thinking was that I withdrew from anything in which I was not strong. The other behavior was to put up a front like I had the answers. In addition to that, I developed a false sense of being superior. Out of that came a penchant for pointing out the faults of others. The list goes on.

When I got into the healing ministry, I tended to take pride in what I did when someone got healed. If they did not get healed, I tended to judge that the person I prayed over was the problem. I decided that they either did not have enough faith or they were not being honest, or they were very private and, as such, they were withholding information that was pertinent to what we were trying to heal.

All of this kind of thinking was really rooted in self-righteousness and a false sense of being superior. One of the behavior patterns I had that helped me realize my false sense of security was that I would ask God to send people for prayer that had the same problem as those who had gotten healed when I prayed over them. In that way, I would know "exactly" how to pray so I could see them healed as well. God never honored that kind of request. The song that Frank Sinatra sang that helped make it popular was "I Did It My Way."

When interacting with the Spirit of God, **doing it my way** does not work. Furthermore, I would try to emulate what I observed (often on TV) were the actions of some of the well-known people in the healing ministry, such as televangelist Benny Hinn. I tried to figure out how he got so many people to end up on the floor when he waved his hand at the crowd.

I cannot even begin to tell you how often I would think or say to myself, "If I were God, this is how I would handle a situation." It became pretty clear that God had his own plans. All that I just talked about were examples of operating in the flesh.

I began to notice that if I prayed over someone and I had no idea what to pray for, I became more dependent upon God to lead me. When I was able to do that, positive results showed up more often. It took me a while, but slowly I realized I am just an instrument that God chooses to use in certain situations. In order to do that, I have to continually hold onto a mindset that I am the tool, or the deliverer of a message and not the person who has the answers. I found that the more time I spent in prayer and in reading the Bible, God's power showed up in a deeper way. This is not a one time, now I get it, kind of thing. I have to continually stop listening to myself, thinking I know how to pray for someone.

One of the biggest hurdles for me is to get out of the mode of being right. When we were in a leadership role in the Marriage Encounter movement, we came to realize it is better to be in a relationship with someone than it is to be right. When I think I am right about something, I cannot hear the other person and I certainly cannot hear God. I mean, in my mind I am right. So why do I need another input on the subject? After all, when I am right, I think I stand in power.

One of the biggest blocks to allowing oneself to be weak so that the Spirit of God can move in with His power is when I am angry. We see it all the time whereby people are angry, because they have been hurt, and they either deny they are angry or they know they are angry and will not move toward letting go of the anger by forgiving the other person or persons.

I have looked back at my life over the years and I have come to realize that every time I made a decision while I was angry, I lost. By that I mean I made the wrong decision. When I am angry there is no place for God's power to operate through me.

In my book, "A Better Way," I delve deeply into anger and what it does to a person, particularly to a relationship with another person. I found, for example, that oftentimes when I was angry with one or more of our children, I needed to get rid of my anger before I tried to deal with their behavior. Many times, my anger was not rooted in their behavior, but rather in my behavior when I was their age. I discovered that when I allowed God to heal my wounds from the time period when I was growing up, I could more lovingly and successfully deal with any behavior in them that I deemed to be wrong. This is particularly true in fathers relating to their children. The scriptures actually call out the behavior of fathers with their children.

Ephesians 6:4

[4] Fathers, do not provoke your children to anger, but bring them up with the training and instruction of the Lord.

Colossians 3:21

[21] Fathers, do not provoke your children, so they may not become discouraged.

So, perhaps, if you have rebellious children maybe it would be best to consider your own behavior and take corrective action such as asking your child for forgiveness rather than stand on the "I am right and you are the problem" platform.

I want to tell one story whereby I did provoke my teenage son. The story entails the living out of the following scripture from Matthew 5:39.

[39] But I say to you, offer no resistance to one who is evil. **When someone strikes you on [your] right cheek, turn the other one to him as well.**

This is not about someone who is evil, but rather it is about turning the other cheek.

It was during a time period when I was still recovering from deep depression. I still had a lot of anger and it did not take much to trigger my anger. We were trying to move our baby grand piano, with me on one side and my teenage son on the other side. I don't remember what was said, but I heard what I thought was a sarcastic response to something coming from my son. In my anger, I tried to reach across the piano to take a swing at him. I not only missed but I experienced a lot of pain as I apparently had some bursitis in that shoulder. My son stepped out from behind the piano and got face to face with me and said, "Dad, if it will make you better, go ahead and beat the [bleep] out of me."

That action totally disarmed me and I think a lot of my anger drained away. I was filled with sorrow and I never raised my hand to anyone again.

That is an example of the power of God's word when it is lived out.

In Matthew 5:23-24 it tells us:

23 Therefore, if you bring your gift to the altar, and there recall that your brother has anything against you, 24 leave your gift there at the altar, go first and be reconciled with your brother, and then come and offer your gift.

Only in this case, substitute "child" for "brother."

I have come to realize that when my mindset is that of seeing God as an awesome God (Fear of the Lord), then it almost becomes natural to accept my being weak. This is not a panicky kind of weakness, but rather it is a comfortable kind of weakness whereby I know God is in charge.

CHAPTER 14

WE APPARENTLY HAVE TWO ANGELS

I have to tell this story and you can interpret it as you are moved to do so.

Many years ago, my wife was attending a Jazzercise Class and during the break she was talking to another woman. She was telling the other woman about the ministry we had pertaining to forgiveness and healing. The woman then told my wife that her daughter and son-in-law and their two children lived in a house where strange and eerie things were happening. During the night they sometimes heard dishes rattling. At times the light fixture over their dining room table would sway back and forth. This kind of phenomenon is called "poltergeist." The lady asked my wife if we dealt with this kind of situation. My wife told her that we did.

When she came home, she told me about the conversation and that she was arranging for an evening where we would go to the house in question. My wife remembers we (she) had asked a priest to go with us. I don't remember that being the case but I have to admit it was probably a good idea. The evening we went to the house the priest had to cancel. So, we went alone. When we got into our car my wife asked me if I knew how to deal with such a thing. I told her I did not know how to deal with it, so we would simply have to rely on the Holy Spirit to guide us. This is a perfect example of being weak. In actuality, relying on the Holy Spirit was our normal mode of operation. But this time we were about to confront something we had never confronted before.

When we got to their home, we introduced ourselves and told them a little bit about our ministry (which had nothing to do with poltergeist). We asked questions like, "Had they had their house blessed?" I don't remember their answer. In any case, we had brought Holy Water with us and suggested we start by going through each room in the house praying a blessing.

The last room we got to was the master bedroom. The married couple indicated that the entire family had become very fearful and that all four of them were sleeping in their king-sized bed. My first thought was that it was probably not too good for their marriage to be doing this.

When I began to pray for a blessing in the room, I received what I will call a word of knowledge from the Holy Spirit. I just spoke what the Holy Spirit was telling me. It went something like this:

I said that there was a spirit of a little girl present in the house. The little girl had died in the house and her spirit was afraid to leave. I was amazed by what came out of my mouth after that.

I said, "Little girl, Jesus is calling you to come home to Him and I know you are afraid to leave. Consequently, I am going to make you part of God's family. Before I do that, since I do not know your name, I am going to give you a baptismal name. Her name is Mary. Mary was the mother of Jesus." I then raised the holy water and baptized her in the name of the Father and the Son and the Holy Spirit. I then told her she was now a member of God's family. I told her to not be afraid as there were two angels waiting to take her to Jesus. I told her God speed and that I would meet her when I got there. At that point I knew we had accomplished what we came to do. So, we said our goodbyes and left for home.

A couple of weeks later, the lady informed my wife that the dish rattling and the light fixture swaying had ceased the night we were there and her family was sleeping well.

I will interject my own thoughts here regarding the death of the little girl. She could have been a baby that had actually been born before she died, or she could have died as a result of a miscarriage. I believe that there are many people who have had miscarriages and never think to give the child a name.

From the moment I said it, I wondered why I told her that there were two angels waiting to take her to Jesus. I never talked about it with anyone, I just carried the question in my heart for years.

Fifteen or twenty years later, a friend of mine invited me to join him in attending Christians in Commerce, a movement that had been around for years. I accepted the invitation and began attending meetings once a week at a local church. Shortly after I joined Christians in Commerce, they announced there was a retreat coming up called the Challenge Weekend. It sounded interesting so I decided to attend.

On that particular weekend, there was a guest speaker who was a retired minister. He and his wife had moved to the east coast to be near their grandchildren. In any case, the speaker talked about what I will call a "special gift," in that he was able to see angels. He told some very interesting stories about what he had observed. He then told us that we all have two angels. He said one angel stays with us and the other angel keeps leaving and coming back. He wondered if the second angel was reporting to a higher angel. In any case, his witness about the two angels satisfied my curiosity as to why I had told Mary that two angels were present to take her to Heaven.

While reading the scriptures recently I came across the following in John 20:11-12:

*¹¹ But Mary stayed outside the tomb weeping. And as she wept, she bent over into the tomb ¹² and saw **two angels** in white sitting there, one at the head and one at the feet where the body of Jesus had been.*

Is the fact that Mary saw two angels in the tomb where Jesus had been laid a coincidence or is it related to what came out of my mouth while speaking the word of knowledge in the incident stated above?

CHAPTER 15

LET HE WHO IS WITHOUT SIN CAST THE FIRST STONE

Have you ever made a mistake in your lifetime that affected other people? If your answer is "NO" you probably won't get much out of this chapter. Before you skip to the next chapter let me ask you if you have ever been annoyed with someone else who made a mistake that caused you some inconvenience? If your answer is "YES" then you might get something out of this chapter.

I love to tell what I call a "living version" of the story that is told in the Gospel of John 8:2-11:

² But early in the morning he arrived again in the temple area, and all the people started coming to him, and he sat down and taught them. ³ Then the scribes and the Pharisees brought a woman who had been caught in adultery and made her stand *in the middle. ⁴ They said to him, "Teacher, this woman was caught in the very act of committing adultery. ⁵ Now in the law, Moses commanded us to stone such women.* So what do you say?" ⁶ They said this to test him, so that they could have some charge to bring against him. Jesus bent down and began to write on the ground with his finger. ⁷ But when they continued asking him, he straightened up and said to them,* **"Let the one among you who is without sin be the first to throw a stone at her."** *⁸ Again he bent down and wrote on the ground. ⁹ And in response, they went away one by one, beginning with the elders. So he was left alone with the woman before him. ¹⁰ Then Jesus straightened up and said to her, "Woman, where are they? Has no one condemned you?" ¹¹ She replied, "No one, sir." Then Jesus said, "Neither do I condemn you. Go, [and] from now on do not sin anymore."*

The story I am about to tell you is NOT about someone who committed adultery. Rather, the story is about someone who made a mistake that resulted in a group of people being disrupted by this person's mistake.

While at work one day I asked our secretary to schedule a meeting for 8-10 people in one of the conference rooms. It just so happened we were working in a building that hosted several different divisions of the company we worked for. When we got to the conference room, it was already occupied by a group from another division. This meant we had to reschedule our meeting. So, we headed back to our secretary's desk to request another time to meet.

When we reached our secretary's desk, I told her what had happened. She apologized immediately indicating she did not know what went wrong. Knowing some of the other people were quite upset and had expressed negative things about the secretary, I simply said, "Anyone who has never made a mistake please feel free to speak now." One by one they all walked away, not saying a word. I thanked the secretary for her hard work and asked her to find an available conference room for us to meet later in the day or the next day.

A scripture that fits in very well for this situation comes from Matthew 7:1-5:

*¹ **"Stop judging**, that you may not be judged. ² For as you judge, so will you be judged, and the measure with which you measure will be measured out to you. ³ Why do you notice the splinter in your brother's eye, **but do not perceive the wooden beam in your own eye?** ⁴ How can you say to*

your brother, 'Let me remove that splinter from your eye,' while the wooden beam is in your eye?
*⁵ **You hypocrite, remove the wooden beam from your eye first;** then you will see clearly to remove the splinter from your brother's eye.*

It is clear that we are to not judge others. We are not talking about things like performance evaluations or raising children. Even with raising children, there are so many parents that expect perfection in the behavior of their children while their own behavior is not that great. Oftentimes, critical judgement of others comes out of one's own failures earlier in life. What we are talking about is things like judging the behavior of other people by holding them to a standard that you yourself don't live. Remember, the call of the Christian is to love others as you love yourself. This is an area where it is so easy to look at the fault of the other person and never even notice your own shortcomings.

CHAPTER 16

THE TRUTH WILL SET YOU FREE

In the Gospel of John, chapter 8:31-32, Jesus implores us to live our lives directed by His Word and, if we do so, the truth of the Word will set us free.

31Jesus then said to those Jews who believed in him, **"If you remain in my word, you will truly be my disciples, 32 and you will know the truth, and the truth will set you free."**

Also, in the Gospel of John, chapter 14:6 Jesus tells us He is the truth.

6 Jesus said to him, **"I am the way and the truth and the life.** *No one comes to the Father except through me."*

The truth that sets one free is Jesus. When we apply faith to His teachings, that is when we live like it says to live and we are set free.

The best example I have of this comes from my own life. Before we get into it, I want to tell you very clearly, I am not holding the other person responsible for what I experience. When one is in a relationship, we have choices as to how to react or deal with what the other person does. I have been around people whose behavior just really bugs me. Sitting right next to that person who bugs me might be someone who is head over heels in love with the person and sees that person differently. The point I am trying to make is we need to look at what is there in me that sees the other person as annoying rather than expect the person who bugs me to change their behavior just so I feel better.

When I was born, my mother was apparently dealing with lots of health issues. Those issues included a myriad of emotional issues. In any case, my father told me one evening after my mother had died, that she, my mother, was not capable of taking care of me for the first three years of my life. When I asked who took care of me, he told me that my Aunt Elsie, my mother's younger sister, came every day and took care of me. Without getting into any more details, I grew up with some sort of emotional pain when it came to relating to my mother. In fact, I thought there was something wrong with me in that I loved my Aunt Elsie more than I loved my mother. I lived many years with this pain that I could not describe. Perhaps one could call the pain a deep sense of emptiness.

I heard a teaching by an ordained minister on the subject he called "call no one on earth your father." When he announced the subject, I thought here it comes, he will attack the fact that people of the Catholic Faith call their priests Father. He never even mentioned the subject. What he did teach was that the title "Father" in this sense, meant the person from whom you came forth.

Psalm 139 tells us that it was God who created us in our mother's womb. We come forth from God. That makes Him our Father. He went on to say that what God creates is good and God does not make mistakes. He went even further to tell us, also from Psalm 139, that God's precious thoughts toward us outnumber the sands.

While attending a tent revival meeting prior to hearing the above stated teaching, I walked up to one of the speakers to thank him for the teaching he had just given us. I don't remember the subject of that teaching but I told the speaker I thought I had a lot to unlearn. He gently expressed frustration, telling me he has people tell him that quite frequently. He said, "You do not have to unlearn anything. Just start living what the Word of God tells you."

I applied that to my life and decided it was true that God created me in my mother's womb and what he creates is wonderful. Furthermore, I bask in the fact that God has endless precious thoughts toward me.

One day I realized I no longer have painful emotional memories with regards to my relationship with my mother. I have been set free by the truth that I am God's creation.

Another example I have had to deal with is how I deal with and how I've dealt with money. There were two major things that happened to me with regards to the handling of money. One had to do with a vow I made to myself regarding frivolous spending. I will talk about that in the next chapter. The other was our decision to tithe. I talked about that in chapter 6, "What is Faith?" The point is that when I started to live as the word of God calls me to live regarding the handling of money, the struggles I was having went away.

CHAPTER 17

MAKING VOWS

Years ago, friends of ours sent us a teaching they had heard about the subject of making vows. There are two scriptures that make reference to the subject. They are:

Matthew 5:33-37

*33 "Again you have heard that it was said to your ancestors, 'Do not take a false oath, but make good to the Lord all that you vow.' 34 But I say to you, do not swear at all; not by heaven, for it is God's throne; 35 nor by the earth, for it is his footstool; nor by Jerusalem, for it is the city of the great King. 36 Do not swear by your head, for you cannot make a single hair white or black. 37 Let your 'Yes' mean 'Yes,' and your 'No' mean 'No.' **Anything more is from the evil one.***

James 5:12

¹² But above all, my brothers, do not swear, either by heaven or by earth or with any other oath, but let your "Yes" mean "Yes" and your "No" mean "No," **that you may not incur condemnation.**

I decided to pray and ask God how this subject of making vows applied to my life. What came to mind were two different instances where I apparently made a vow and those vows were affecting my relationship with other people, particularly my wife and my children. One was related to my relationship with my mother-in-law. That also carried over to my relationship with my family members.

When I was young and our family moved from suburbia to the farm, it was not long before we were in the state of barely making ends meet. I remember my parents fought a lot about money and frivolous spending. During this time period, I apparently made a vow to never spend money frivolously. When we got married, I found I could not allow myself to spend money on anything but what was needed. This caused a lot of tension in our family relationship.

The kinds of things I am talking about was that I would not allow myself to buy nice jewelry for Anita despite the fact that we could afford it. I would get upset when she wanted to have her nails done. I could not accept expensive gifts from Anita. One year, way before the cell phone was in existence, Anita got me a CB radio for my pickup truck. I made her take it back. When I heard in my spirit that I had made this vow and that it clearly created problems, I repented and I took the matter to a priest in confession.

The other vow that was detrimental to our family relationship had to do with my relationship with my mother-in-law. When my wife and I were dating, I sensed that my mother-in-law would have preferred her daughter to marry someone of the same faith and who could provide more money. I was going to be a school teacher and I think she thought a doctor or lawyer would be better suited for her daughter. I have to say I don't really know if this is how she saw things.

The point was it was in my head and I had no idea how to approach the subject with her. The night we got married my mother-in-law told me I could call her "Mother." At the time I did not see this as perhaps her way of welcoming me into the family. After all, I had my own view of the subject. Consequently, under my breath, I told myself I would never call her mother.

Years later, when I tried to reverse that, the words just stuck in my throat. Here too, I took the fact that

I had made such a vow to the confessional. While in confession, I asked the priest to pray for me to be freed from the vows I had made. When he prayed, I felt like chains around my chest had been broken. I was free to allow myself to spend money in a more loving fashion. I asked my mother-in-law for forgiveness and she not only forgave me but she told me she had come to love being called Nana. It was the beginning of a more loving relationship with her. For more details, I wrote about this subject in my book entitled, "A Better Way."

Here are a couple of scriptures from the Old Testament regarding the act of making a vow.

Numbers 30:3

³ When a man makes a vow to the LORD or binds himself under oath to a pledge, he shall not violate his word, but must fulfill exactly the promise he has uttered.

Deuteronomy 23:22-24

²² When you make a vow to the LORD, your God, you shall not delay in fulfilling it; for the LORD, your God, will surely require it of you and you will be held guilty. ²³ Should you refrain from making a vow, you will not be held guilty. ²⁴ But whatever your tongue utters you must be careful to do, just as you freely vowed to the LORD, your God, with your own mouth.

Ecclesiastes 5:3-4

³ When you make a vow to God, delay not its fulfillment. For God has no pleasure in fools; fulfill what you have vowed. ⁴ It is better not to make a vow than to make it and not fulfill it.

CHAPTER 18

HONOR FATHER AND MOTHER

I chose to include a chapter about honoring father and mother because I saw the fallout effect honoring father and mother had on our family. In talking about the practice of honoring father and mother with other Christians I got the sense from some, not all, that they believed honoring father and mother was for children and not for adults. One man even told me, "You don't owe your parents anything. After all, you did not ask to be brought into this world." I have to say I responded to that attitude by asking him, "What Gospel do they read in your church?"

As I have gotten older, I am noticing more and more families where the elders are not particularly honored and in some cases their children have little or no relationship with their parents, grandparents, etc.

When I scanned the Bible, I was surprised to see how many scripture verses talked about honoring father and mother. I am including some of those scriptures just to give you a flavor of what God's Word says.

Exodus 20:12

¹² Honor your father and your mother, ***that you may have a long life in the land the LORD your God is giving you.***

Deuteronomy 5:15-16

¹⁵ Remember that you too were once slaves in the land of Egypt, and the LORD, your God, brought you out from there with a strong hand and outstretched arm. That is why the LORD, ***your God, has commanded you to observe the sabbath day.*** *¹⁶* ***Honor your father and your mother, as the LORD, your God, has commanded you, that you may have a long life and that you may prosper in the land the LORD your God is giving you.***

Isn't it interesting that the command to honor the Sabbath and to honor father and mother are mentioned in the same breath? Also notice God tells us that when you do honor your father and mother you will **prosper** in the land God gives you. Prosper in this sense is not limited to monetary gains. You will prosper in your relationships as well.

Matthew 15:1-6

*¹ Then Pharisees and scribes came to Jesus from Jerusalem and said, ² "Why do your disciples break the tradition of the elders? They do not wash [their] hands when they eat a meal." **³ He said to them in reply, "And why do you break the commandment of God for the sake of your tradition? ⁴ For God said, 'Honor your father and your mother,' and 'Whoever curses father or mother shall die.' ⁵ But you say, 'Whoever says to father or mother, "Any support you might have had from me is dedicated to God," ⁶ need not honor his father.' You have nullified the Word of God for the sake of your tradition.***

Now those are pretty strong words.

Matthew 19:16-18

*¹⁶ Now someone approached him and said, "Teacher, what good must I do to gain eternal life?" ¹⁷ He answered him, "Why do you ask me about the good? There is only One who is good. **If you wish to enter into life, keep the commandments." ¹⁸ He asked him, "Which ones?"** And Jesus* *replied, "You shall not kill; you shall not commit adultery; you shall not steal; you shall not bear false witness; 19 **honor your father and your mother'**; and you shall love your neighbor as yourself."*

Here, too, honoring father and mother is right up there with, "Do not kill, don't commit adultery, etc."

Ephesians 6:1-3

*[1] Children, obey your parents [in the Lord], for this is right. [2] **"Honor your father and mother." This is the first commandment with a promise,** [3] **"that it may go well with you and that you may have a long life on earth."***

When I was reading the book of Exodus in the 21st chapter, I came across two verses that really seem to put God's view of how we treat our parents into perspective.

In the 15th verse it says:

[15] Whoever strikes father or mother shall be put to death.

In the 17th verse it says:

[17] *Whoever curses father or mother shall be put to death.*

I had one man tell me honoring father and mother in his family did not work. Well, God does not break His promises. So, if you are having doubts about things God promises I suggest you look elsewhere, not at God. Elsewhere should begin with the log in one's own eye.

In their later years, my parents lived in a mobile home less than a mile from our house and Anita's mother lived very close to the church we attended. Essentially, every Sunday we spent time with Anita's mother at and after church and then we went to my parents' home for lunch with our children. When my mother had a stroke and had to be moved to a nursing facility, Anita invited my father over for dinner virtually every evening and her mother joined us as well. I found it interesting that people from our church would tell Anita that she did not have to do that. After all, we had our own lives.

I have to tell you that during the months that both grandparents came to dinner we watched our children change. And I should add that at least three of the children were teenagers during this time. The grandparents often told stories from their earlier life and we all listened with much enjoyment. When they each died, the children told some amazing stories of how they had come to love them. Our son surprised everyone when he told stories of how he would take his Nana out for ice cream, even though she was not supposed to have it and how he grew close to both of them.

Today we have found that our children have carried the practice of honoring mother and father into their own families. I was blown away at a recent family reunion, which I attended despite having back spasms. What blew me away was that every time I moved to get up, two or three of the teenagers jumped up to help me without any prompting from their parents. One day my back was really hurting so I elected to stay close to our room. The teens came down several times bringing games to play. We are truly blessed.

CHAPTER 19

REJOICE ALWAYS

I know this has been cited earlier in this book, but I am going to reference it again. In 1 Thessalonians 5:16-18 the scriptures tell us to rejoice always.

16 **Rejoice always**. *17 Pray without ceasing. 18* **In all circumstances give thanks**, *for this is the will of God for you in Christ Jesus.*

Saint Paul also tell us in Philippians 4:4-7,

4 Rejoice in the Lord always. I shall say it again: rejoice! 5 Your kindness should be known to all. The Lord is near. 6 Have no anxiety at all, but in everything, by prayer and petition, with thanksgiving, make your requests known to God. 7 Then the peace of God that surpasses all understanding will guard your hearts and minds in Christ Jesus.[f]

How can that be? I mean there are so many circumstances where rejoicing seems out of order. It is out of order when someone hurts you deeply. It is out of order when your spouse runs off with another person. It is out of order when someone attacks your daughter and the doctors tell you she will likely never walk again.

The first question one needs to ask one's self is, "Can I fix the problem?" Killing or maiming the person who hurts you does not fix the problem. It makes it worse. Staying angry does not fix the problem. So, why is God telling us to always rejoice?

Let's begin with who we are. God knew us before the world began (Ephesians 1:3-4), God created us in our mother's womb, and He does not make mistakes (Psalm 139:13-14). In fact, I suggest you read all of Psalms 139 and realize His precious thoughts for us outnumber the sands. It goes on and on. God is adopting us as one of His children and we do not have to do anything to earn it except to believe it. See Galatians 3:26. We are saved by grace (we have salvation), we do not have to do anything but believe it (faith). See Ephesians 2:4-9.

Now, here is a great big reason why we are called to **rejoice always**. God will turn all things together that happen to you to good. If you believe what the scripture says about what is good for you, and in believing you live it (see Romans 8:28).

One of the stumbling blocks we can get into is when we decide what is good, that is, we decide what should happen. The stumbling block comes from our fleshly view of things in which we think we know what is right for each situation. God sees the bigger picture and we have to yield to that. So, the faith we have should not be used to get things "my way." The faith in the situation is that we know God will do what is best. We can do that when we see God as awesome (Fear of the Lord).

Let me give you a couple of examples that occurred in our lives or in the lives of people we know.

A friend came to us for counseling and prayer. Her husband had left her and was now living with a younger woman. She could not sleep and was losing weight because she had no desire to eat. We showed her that in Luke 6:27 and on (you might want to read it), to pray for the person that hurt her. We told her to praise God and to ask God to bless her husband right where he was. She told us that she thought we were crazy, but would do as we suggested.

A week or two later she came back and said she was sleeping a little better but was still not eating, etc. We told her to continue praising and thanking

God while the situation continued and to ask God to bless the other woman. In other words, we told her she needed to forgive them both, and by asking God to bless them she was walking in the right direction (that is also God's will for her). She said again that she thought we were really crazy, but agreed to pray for her as well. A week or two later her husband came home and asked to be reconciled. They reconciled and they are still married, more than 30 years later.

I have always wanted to attend a football game at the University of Notre Dame. A friend told us we should get there a day early to attend the pep rally as well. Our granddaughter was attending Notre Dame and her dad arranged for us to meet them there to go to the pep rally and attend a game. We were pretty excited. One of our daughters happened to be attending a conference in Chicago that week and asked to be included. She said she would meet us at the airport in Chicago and we would move on to South Bend together. We got up at 4:00 A.M. to catch an early flight to Chicago. We checked in at the airport in plenty of time.

While eating breakfast at the airport, I got a text that our flight had been canceled. We were told to reschedule another flight. While standing in line we were held off to the side while they checked in passengers for their flights that morning. This was a real opportunity for me to get angry about the whole situation. Instead of getting angry, I chose to rejoice at what was happening and stood there praising God. To make a long story short, we finally got on a plane for Chicago, but the new plane would arrive in Chicago some four or five hours later than the original flight. More rejoicing! Our daughter met us in baggage claim and assured us she would figure out how to get us to South Bend. She told me specifically to let her figure out how we would do that. Well, we walked around the baggage claim area in circles as she could not make up her mind as to what to do. More rejoicing. While we were wandering around, my wife got a text from our son that a Jesuit priest who is a friend of his wife's family and was studying at Notre Dame was headed to the airport to pick up his brother. He gave us the priest's phone number which we called. When he answered the phone, he told us he had just arrived and we could ride with him if we could fit in his car. More rejoicing. We picked a door to leave the baggage claim area and lo and behold we picked the right door.

When his brother arrived, we all headed for South Bend. While driving, I learned that both brothers had grown up in a prayer community in El Paso,

Texas. Back in the 1970's, a book called "Miracles in El Paso" had been published chronicling a myriad of miracles that had occurred when this prayer community had decided to feed the poor just across the Mexican border. By miracles I mean things like food multiplied when more people than had been anticipated showed up. It turned out that the priest's brother was still associated with the prayer community.

We had a practice of texting our daughter that lived near us that we had arrived safely at our destination when we traveled. For some reason I got the sense that I should call her while enroute to tell her we were in good hands. In the course of the conversation, I asked our daughter if she remembered the book "Miracles in El Paso." She got really excited when I asked the question because she said that a nun who was living at the parish where she taught religion had just that day received permission from the local bishop to leave the diocese and go to El Paso to join with that prayer community to minister to the poor. The only problem she had was that she had no contact with anyone from that community. I handed my phone to the brother and the problem of the nun having a contact was solved.

In this case, we did not get to the pep rally. In fact, we found out later the pep rally had been canceled because of the weather. However, the fact that God had used us to make the connection for this nun far outweighed going to the pep rally. I cannot even describe the joy I experienced in being used by God in this fashion.

I want to make one other point. Living in faith is not a formula for getting what I want. It is far better than that. It is walking in God's protective grace.

CHAPTER 20

WHERE DO YOU LIVE

A couple of years ago, old friends of ours were in town visiting their daughter. My wife invited them over for lunch on Christmas Eve. That was the only time our schedules matched. It turned out only the wife came over. Her husband did not come because, apparently, he was not feeling well. The daughter did not come because she was in the hospital and was very sick. In the course of the conversation, we learned their daughter was angry with both of her parents and she did not want to see them. I told the mother I would go see her daughter that very afternoon.

While visiting the daughter in the hospital I told her I would like to pray over her. She responded by telling me she did not believe in "that stuff." I told her she did not have to believe. I was the only one who needed to believe. She had five major health problems, and she apparently was very sick.

Quite frankly, I was taken aback when she said she did not believe in healing. The family had lived across the street from us for years and had attended Church pretty much every Sunday.

I probably should not have been surprised by her not believing. In the few years I had been in the healing ministry I was told all kinds of things about healing. Some told me the church they attended taught that Jesus no longer healed, others said that healing had stopped when the apostles had died. Well, we talked about that earlier in the book. Others got angry when I brought up the subject of healing. Some verbally lashed back. My guess (and this guess is an example operating in the flesh) is that they most likely had prayed for a loved one asking God to heal their loved one and their loved one had died anyway.

In any case, I prayed over this young woman and I received notice on Christmas morning that every problem she had had been healed. The hospital ran tests the day after Christmas and confirmed she was indeed healed.

The title of this chapter is not asking for your address. The title of this chapter is meant to lead you into which Kingdom you choose to live. In the Gospel of Matthew, Jesus is speaking to the multitudes when he broaches the subject of prayer. In growing up in our particular faith, we have been taught to memorize this prayer, to recite this prayer, etc. In fact, the prayer I am talking about might just be the most familiar prayer in all of Christendom. What I am talking about is known as "the Lord's Prayer" or in some churches it is referred to as the "Our Father."

Matthew 6:7-13

7 In praying, do not babble like the pagans, who think that they will be heard because of their many words. 8 Do not be like them. **Your Father knows what you need before you ask him.** *9 "This is how you are to pray: Our Father in heaven, hallowed be your name, 10* **your kingdom come, your will be done, on earth as in heaven.** *11* **Give us today our daily bread;** *12 and forgive us our debts, as we forgive our debtors; 13 and do not subject us to the final test, but deliver us from the evil one.*

The New King James version uses language that I find more comfortable to read. It also has wording that extends verse 13 to include: *"For Yours is the kingdom and the power and the glory forever."*

⁷ And when you pray, do not use vain repetitions as the heathen do. For they think that they will be heard for their many words. ⁸ Therefore do not be like them. **For your Father knows the things you need before you ask Him.** *⁹ In this manner, therefore, pray: Our Father in heaven, Hallowed be Your name.* **¹⁰ Your kingdom come. You will be done On earth as it is in heaven. ¹¹ Give us this day our daily bread.** *¹² And forgive us our debts, As we forgive our debtors. ¹³ And do not lead us into temptation, But deliver us from the evil one. For Yours is the kingdom and the power and the glory forever. Amen.*

Why the Catholic Bible differs from most other versions of the Bible, by eliminating those last words, I do not know, nor is it the intention of this book to go down that road.

For the purpose of this discussion, let's focus on verse 10, which I highlighted in **bold**.

I think it is fair to say that each person has created some form of their own kingdom in which they live. Jesus tells us the kingdom of God (heaven, as stated in verse 10 above) is where we should be living.

What is interesting to me is the Lord's Prayer is recited (prayed) over and over again, yet I wonder how many people understand that it includes asking God to bring His Kingdom to earth without any idea what that means.

I think we can agree there is no sickness in heaven. So, by praying that God's Kingdom comes to earth just like it is in heaven, we are asking God for healing to manifest on earth.

In verse 11, above, the Lord's Prayer talks about **our daily bread**. I always thought about the bread that feeds our flesh. Most of us actually feed our flesh at least three times a day, more if we snack. The question is, how often do we feed our spirit with the word of God? During the years I did not attend any church, the answer was not at all. Attending church once a week pretty much equates to feeding our spirit weekly. I think this points out that we truly need to be reading God's word or listen to it being preached every day.

Hebrews 13:7-9

*7 Remember your leaders who spoke the word of God to you. Consider the outcome of their way of life and imitate their faith. 8 **Jesus Christ is the same yesterday, today, and forever.** 9 **Do not be carried away by all kinds of strange teaching**. It is good to have our hearts strengthened by grace and not by foods, which do not benefit those who live by them.*

Verse 8, above, clearly speaks to healing among other things. Jesus was a healer while on earth. He received that power when He was baptized in the Holy Spirit. Since healing had gone away for centuries and then "suddenly" started up again in the late 1800's, I wonder if the fact that occurred after so many years could be conceived as a "strange teaching" as talked about in verse 9. I mean we as humans, when operating in the flesh, surely do not like our kingdom rocked by a new phenomenon, such as people being healed by someone praying over that person.

Let's talk about the Kingdom of God.

Romans 14:17

[17] **For the kingdom of God** is not a matter of food and drink, **but of righteousness, peace, and joy in the holy Spirit;**

What this tells us is that the Kingdom of God comes to us in the spirit, not in the flesh.

1 Corinthians 4:20

[20] *For the kingdom of God is not a matter of talk **but of power.***

Here we are told again that the Kingdom of God is where we receive God's power. That happens in the spirit, the matter of talk is about the flesh. The power comes from the Holy Spirit.

1 Corinthians 15:50:

⁵⁰ This I declare, brothers: **flesh and blood cannot inherit the kingdom of God,** nor does corruption inherit incorruption.

Verse 50 of 1 Corinthians chapter 15 clearly states we cannot inherit the Kingdom of God when we operate in the flesh (in other words without the Holy Spirit).

Be honest with yourself, where do you live?

How do we enter the Kingdom of God?

Matthew 6:33 tells us:

³³ *But seek first the kingdom [of God] and his righteousness, and all these things will be given you besides.*

We need to seek the Kingdom of God.

Mark 10:15 tells us:

¹⁵ Amen, I say to you, **whoever does not accept the kingdom of God like a child will not enter it."**

Accepting like a child means we see God as awesome and we just trust like a child trusts his father, and we jump in.

I find Luke 7:28 very interesting, as is Luke 9:62:

²⁸ I tell you, among those born of women, no one is greater than John; yet the least in the kingdom of God is greater than he."

⁶²[To him] Jesus said, "No one who sets a hand to the plow and looks to what was left behind is fit for the kingdom of God."

It looks like an all or nothing proposition. One cannot expect to enter the kingdom of God while still hanging onto the kingdom they set up for themselves.

In the Gospel of John 3:3-5, the kingdom of God is referenced twice.

*³ Jesus answered and said to him, "Amen, amen, I say to you, **no one can see the kingdom of God without being born from above**." ⁴ Nicodemus said to him, "How can a person once grown old be born again? Surely, he cannot reenter his mother's womb and be born again, can he?" ⁵ Jesus answered, "Amen, amen, I say to you, **no one can enter the kingdom of God without being born of water and Spirit.***

In the Acts of the Apostles Chapter 14:22 we are told one will go through many tribulations to enter the kingdom of God.

*22 They strengthened the spirits of the disciples and exhorted them **to persevere in the faith**, saying, **"It is necessary for us to undergo many hardships to enter the kingdom of God."***

CHAPTER 21

SEEK ME FIRST

Throughout history God has laid down a certain premise; he will not "force himself upon us" but rather he wants us to seek him. I truly believe that is a facet of love. Love would not be love if one were not given free will.

The following are just a few scriptures that speak that message to us.

Zachariah 1:3

³ Say to them: Thus says the LORD of hosts, **return to me***—oracle of the LORD* of hosts—***and I will return to you, says the LORD of hosts.**

Malachi 3:7

⁷ Since the days of your ancestors you have turned aside from my statutes and have not kept them.

Return to me, that I may return to you, says the LORD of hosts. *But you say, "Why should we return?"*

Proverbs 8:17

*¹⁷ Those who love me I also love, and **those who seek me find me.***

Jeremiah 29:12-13

*¹² When you call me, and come and pray to me, I will listen to you. ¹³ **When you look for me, you will find me. Yes, when you seek me with all your heart.***

Amos 5:4

*⁴ For thus says the LORD to the house of Israel: **Seek me, that you may live.***

My wife and I had a lady who came to us over the years for counseling and prayers. She was going through a divorce and was experiencing great emotional pain. We listened to her story and offered to pray over her. We did not consider ourselves as qualified to counsel, other than to try to lead a person into a deeper relationship with the Lord.

During the time we were praying for her, I got the sense that God wanted her to experience His love for her in a deeper way. When we finished praying, I was led to ask her to go into a Catholic church and spend some time before the Blessed Sacrament. Since she was of another faith, I explained to her that she would find the Blessed Sacrament is a box (tabernacle) at the front of the church and would know Christ was present when she saw a red candle holder with a candle that was lit. When she had walked out of our home, my wife questioned me, reminding me she was of another faith. I told her I was just passing along what I heard in my spirit while we were praying.

The lady returned the following week to thank us and said she sat down in the pew in front of the tabernacle where she said she became enveloped in what she described as a warm love that she had never experienced before. She said she wept for an hour. When she left, she was experiencing a great sense of peace. We never saw her again.

Another time we were in San Diego living in our fifth wheel for the summer. We had befriended several couples who also spent the summer in the same trailer park, escaping from the desert heat. One day one of the ladies stopped by and asked us to pray for the other couple as she sensed they were struggling with what they should do about the business they owned, which was apparently in a downturn. When

I prayed for the other couple, I heard in my spirit that God wanted to minister to them, for lack of a better explanation, and He wanted them to come to Him. It just so happened we were meeting with the couple the next evening for dinner.

When we were finishing dinner, I broached the subject. I told them I was praying for them and I heard the Holy Spirit say God wanted to meet with them at His place. I know that is a strange way to express it, but that is what came out of my mouth. She said they prayed every day. I said I can't respond to that but repeated that He wanted them to take the step of coming to Him. She had been raised in the Catholic church but was no longer attending church. He had been raised in another faith and was also not attending church.

I told her she knew where God wanted to meet with them and the next step was up to them. A few weeks later, there was a knock at our door one evening while we were watching TV. They came in very excited to tell us that they had passed a Catholic church late that afternoon and decided to go in and spend some time before the Blessed Sacrament. I asked her what occurred. She said she became filled with peace, peace like she had not experienced for a long time. I asked him what his experience was. He said he felt like he was enveloped in a warm love and he simply cried for the entire time they were there.

Shortly after, they sold their business and retired. We saw them a couple times after that in the next few years and they said they were living in peace and joy.

I have to share one other story about God's desire to have someone return to Him. A friend was suffering from cancer. The suffering continued for months and, if I recall, continued for at least a year or longer. A different friend discerned that we needed to pull together a group of prayerful people who had also labored in the healing ministry. We agreed to have the team assemble in our home and we would pray over the person suffering from cancer for the entire weekend or until the person was healed. We all agreed we would fast the entire weekend and our prayer sessions would take place Friday evening, Saturday evening and Sunday afternoon, if need be.

When the team laid hands on the patient on Friday evening, it was not long before the person manifested an evil spirit or spirits. The spirits would not leave so we got the person back to a normal countenance. The person suffering and the person's spouse became very fearful. When we sent them home, the team agreed to pray for them throughout the night. Since we were all married couples, we assigned an hour or two to each couple and went back to our respective homes and did just that. We had someone praying for the other couple so that they might experience some restful sleep.

When the couple returned Saturday evening for more prayers, the person with the cancer announced they would not allow us to get that close again. This was not a good thing. We prayed that evening with no visible signs of progress. We all went home that night, attended church services in our respected churches and returned Sunday afternoon to continue praying. It was during this time that something very interesting occurred.

After praying for some time, I got up from the group and walked into our kitchen to take a rest and to have a drink of water. Another man from the team followed me into the kitchen to tell me what he had experienced.

He told me that while he was praying, he had a vision. He told me he saw Jesus in a boat and He, Jesus, called out to the person with cancer to come to Him. I suggested we go back into the room to pray, and instructed my friend to very quietly whisper into the ear of the person with the cancer what he had seen. I got down close so I could hear what was being said.

My friend told the person with cancer that he had a vision in which he heard Jesus calling to the person with the cancer to come to Him. He did not mention anything about Jesus being in a boat just off shore. The person with the cancer responded saying he preferred to stay where he was on shore and that he chose to stand behind a boat that was on shore in front of him. The entire scenario boggled my mind. The person with the cancer had said he would not go to Jesus as he had been called. Not a good move. Since it was late in the afternoon, and we were all getting tired I turned to one of the team members and asked him to lead us in some praise music. He picked up his guitar and began to sing "I have decided to follow Jesus."

The only thing I could conclude from that was that Jesus was asking the cancer patient to turn to Him.

We broke for dinner, which my wife had so graciously prepared. When we had eaten and the person with the cancer had left to go home, I polled every team member to express what they had experienced. Pretty much everyone said it was the most spirit filled experience they had ever had.

The person we had prayed over eventually succumbed to the cancer.

CHAPTER 22

SORROW - A KEY INGREDIENT TO REPENTANCE

I continually find our God to be an awesome God in that He seems to use every opportunity to speak to me through His Word on a very personal basis. Recently, while reading God's Word, the following scripture just seems to jump off the pages. That is a signal to me that God wants to speak to me about how the following scripture will deepen my relationship with Him.

The reading I am talking about comes from 2 Corinthians 7:9-10

⁹ I rejoice now, not because you were saddened, but because you were saddened into repentance; for you were saddened in a godly way, so that you did not suffer loss in anything because of us. ¹⁰ For godly sorrow produces a **salutary repentance**

without regret*, but worldly sorrow produces death.*

Allow me to say a few things about what is contained in the scripture. When I was a young boy, before there was a television in almost every household, there was a radio program that I listened to quite often. The program presented comedy revolving around a female "Dennis the Menace" whose name, as was the title of the show, was Baby Snooks. One of the comedy sketches depicted Baby Snooks standing in line at the local bank with her father. In those days the tellers worked behind a barred window. Baby Snooks looked at the teller standing behind the bars and said to her father, "That lady in the cage looks like a horse." The teller responded to the statement by Baby Snooks with a deep voice indicating she was offended by the comment.

Baby Snook's father reprimanded her and told her to apologize.

Baby Snooks responded by telling the teller, "I am sorry that you look like a horse."

That is an exaggerated example of worldly sorrow. The death the scripture associates with worldly sorrow is not physical death but is rather spiritual death as it separates one further from God

Godly sorrow on the other hand produces "salutary repentance without regret." This means it brings us closer to God.

As it turned out, I already had real-life examples of this particular scripture. I have to take you back to the time when I had decided to join my wife in her spiritual journey by joining the Catholic faith. One of the steps we needed to take was to make our first confession. Something which I was not only unfamiliar with but I was also very nervous about taking that step. I was blessed to have been working with a very gentle and truly Holy Man of God.

When I entered the confessional, there was a screen between myself and the priest. I was relieved when the priest asked me if I would like him to guide me through the process. He went through a litany of sinful behavior that made me think he had been following me around for my entire life. It seemed like there was not very much that I said no to. I was truly relieved when it was over.

Now, let's roll forward some 15-20 years. My wife and I had grown children. One day one of our children did something that was outside what we thought was proper behavior. While my wife handled the situation quite lovingly, I found myself very agitated by what had happened and I worked very hard to not react with the anger I was experiencing. I decided to take some time to pray and to ask God for guidance as to what to do.

Much to my surprise, I heard God tell me that He wanted me to go to confession. I kind of argued with God and I told Him I think He got His wires crossed. So, I asked again, and got the same response: go to confession. Well, I finally gave in and said I would go to confession. When I did that, I experienced great peace.

Saturday night came and the Holy Spirit reminded me that I needed to go to the church to meet with the priest. In the confessional, the priest and I sat face to face. When I finished relating what I thought I needed to confess the priest asked me if there was anything else I needed to confess. I started to say no, when the word yes came out of my mouth. I cried as I confessed sinfulness from my teen years. I remember the priest even cried. When I was finished, I left the confessional and knelt to pray and I told God that I had confessed all that stuff in my first confession, so why was I moved to confess it again. He simply told me there was no sorrow the first time I confessed it.

I will end this part of the story by saying that I looked at my daughter's behavior in a totally different way. This time my heart was filled with the love of Christ.

Over the years, in the healing ministry and when observing family situations in general, I have seen the same general scenario of parents being angry with their children's behavior. Oftentimes, that behavior does not line up with the situation. One can pretty much bet that the parents, usually the fathers more than the mothers, are dealing from the position of unmitigated behavior in their own lives. The solution is to deal with this unmitigated behavior before dealing with the children's behavior. I am not saying this is the sole source of the anger, but it sure is a good place to start looking.

One other observation. It seems like the stronger a person's denial is regarding their own behavior, the more likely the behavior exists.

CHAPTER 23

WAKE UP CHURCH

The world is a mess and the church is also a mess. Less than 50% of Christians attend church. In our country, people think the political party they are affiliated with will solve the world's problems. Really?

People are hungry and many of the churches seem to have no idea how to satisfy that hunger. The Bible tells us that the Word of God is what satisfies their hunger. It is the spirit that is not being fed (see chapter 2 of this book).

In many churches they are offering social gatherings to "bring people back." This is good but, in my opinion, people are hungry for spiritual food.

In many cases, people are leaving their church to attend a church where the Word of God is preached and being lived. That should be a hint.

At the last supper, Jesus was praying. Here is part of the prayer from John 17:14-23:

*[14] I gave them **your word**, and the world hated them, because they do not belong to the world any more than I belong to the world. [15] I do not ask that you take them out of the world but that you **keep them from the evil one.** [16] They do not belong to the world any more than I belong to the world. [17] Consecrate them with the truth. **Your word is truth.** [18] As you sent me into the world, so I sent them into the world. [19] And I consecrate myself for them, so that they also may be consecrated in truth. [20] "I pray not only for them, but also for those who **will believe in me through their word,** [21] **so that they may all be one**, as you, Father, are in me and I in you, that they also may be in us, **that the world may believe that you sent me.** [22] And I have given them the glory you gave me, **so that they may be one, as we are one,** [23] I in them and you in me, that they **may be brought to perfection as one, that the world may know that you sent me,** and that you loved them even as you loved me.*

This scripture contains a large part of the answer.

The Word of God must be preached.

We are fighting against the evil one.

One cannot fight against the evil one while operating in the flesh. In fact, none of this can be accomplished in the flesh. This means one must be operating in the Spirit. That tells me that the baptism in the Holy Spirit is paramount.

The early church preached the word and they baptized all in the Holy Spirit. It is not an option.

The other message is a call to unity. As long as church members cling to their church's theology and practices and in doing so deny or impede the call to unity, then the world will not know that God sent Jesus into the world. Is that where we stand today? The first chapter of the gospel of John tells us that Jesus is the **Word** made flesh.

In 2 Chronicles 7:14, God calls us to humble ourselves and to pray.

14 If then my people, upon whom my name has been pronounced, ***humble themselves and pray****, and seek my face and turn from their evil ways, I will hear them from heaven and* ***pardon their sins and heal their land.***

Our God is a God of love who sent His only son through whom we have forgiveness of sins and through whom we have been reconciled to the Father. **He gave us His Word.**

ABOUT THE AUTHOR

Ron and his wife, Anita, have been married for over 62 years. They met in college when they were both 17. They have four children, ten grandchildren and one great grandson. At one time they were coordinators of the Southwest for World Wide Marriage Encounter. They then moved into the healing ministry where they labored for over 30 years. They have spoken on the subjects of forgiveness and healing, marriage, family, and parenting at various churches and conventions in the states of Arizona, California, Oregon, Washington, Nevada, Utah, New Mexico and as far east as Ohio. This is Ron's second book, the first being "A Better Way".

APPENDIX A SCRIPTURE REFERENCES BY CHAPTER

Introduction
    Matthew 13:44-46

Chapter 1 The Original Motivation Behind Writing This Book
    Hebrews 4:12
    Matthew 1
    Philippians 2:5-11

Chapter 2 The Lifegiving Nature of God's Word
    Deuteronomy 8:3
    Matthew 4:4
    Luke 4:4
    Proverbs 14:12
    Proverbs 16:25

Chapter 3 Understanding Our Identity Through Christ
    Ephesians 1:4
    Romans 8:14-16

Galatians 3:26
Ephesians 2:4-9
Exodus 15:2
2 Samuel 22:3
2 Samuel 22:47
Psalms 13:6
Psalms 62:7
Micah 7:7
Luke 3:5-6
Ephesians 1:13
1 Peter 1:8-9
Revelation 19:1
John 17:20-21

Chapter 4 We Have an Awesome God

Psalms 138:1-8
Nehemiah 1:5
Daniel 9:4
Deuteronomy 10:21
Job 37:22
Psalms 147:5
James 2:14-26
Psalms 111:10
Proverbs 1:7

Proverbs 9: 10-11
Proverbs 1:20-30
Proverbs 2:1-15
Hosea 4:6
Proverbs 10: 27
Proverbs 14: 26-27
Proverbs 15: 16
Proverbs 15:33
Proverbs 19:23
Proverbs 22: 4
Proverbs 23: 17
Acts of the Apostles 9:31
Psalms 34:2-12

Chapter 5 The Spirit or The Flesh
Ephesians 1:3-6
Psalms 139:13-14
Psalms 139:17-18
Matthew 16:15-16
Matthew 16:22-23
Ephesians 1
Psalms 1:1-3
Psalms 139
1 Corinthians 2:3-5

    1 Corinthians 2:12-14
    Romans 8:1-17
    Galatians 5:1, 13-26

Chapter 6 What is Faith?
    Hebrews 11:1-6
    James 2:14-26
    1 Thessalonians 5:16-18
    Romans 8:28
    1 John 5:3
    Haggai 2:8
    Malachi 3:7-10
    Proverbs 12:14
    Proverbs 16:25
    Matthew 18:20
    1 Thessalonians 2:13

Chapter 7 Hearing God Speak.
    John 10:25-29
    John 8:42-43
    John 14:15-17
    John 6:28-29
    Matthew 10:5-10
    Luke 10:8-9
    John 18:37-38
    1 Kings 17:24

John 14:6
Genesis 1:27
Mark 10:15
1 Kings 19:11-13
Exodus 7:20

Chapter 8 Missing God's Command

1 Thessalonians 5:16-18

Chapter 9 Discerning God's Will

Genesis 1:27
Psalms 139:13-14
2 Timothy 3:16-17
James 1:5-8
1 Thessalonians 5:16-18
Luke 6:30
1 Thessalonians 5:18
Matthew 5:22-24
Matthew 5:3-5
Proverbs 14:12
Proverbs 16:25

Chapter 10 Baptism of the Holy Spirit.

Mark 1:7-11
Luke 24:49
Romans 14:17

1 Corinthians 4:20
1 Corinthians 15:50
Romans 6:11
Acts of the Apostles 19:1-6
John 3:1-7
1 Peter 1:23-25

Chapter 11 Where Did the Power Go?
Matthew 12:24
John 14:12

Chapter 12 Confronting Evil
Ephesians 6:10-12
1 Peter 5:25-27
Ephesians 4:6-9
John 10:10
Matthew 12:43-45
Luke 11:24-26
Mark 5:6-10
Luke 8:30
John 10:10

Chapter 13 When I am Weak is When I am Strong
2 Corinthians 12:8-10
Ephesians 6:4
Colossians 3:21
Matthew 5:23-24

Chapter 14 We Apparently Have Two Angels.
John 20:11-12

Chapter 15 Let He Who Is Without Sin Cast the First Stone.
John 8:2-11
Matthew 7:1-5

Chapter 16 The Truth Will Set You Free
John 8:31-32
Psalms 139

Chapter 17 Making Vows
Matthew 5:33-37
James 5:12
Numbers 3:23-30
Deuteronomy 23:22-24
Ecclesiastes 5:3-4

Chapter 18 Honor Father and Mother
Exodus 20:12
Deuteronomy 5:15-16
Matthew 15:1-6
Matthew 19:16-18
Ephesians 6:1-3
Exodus 21:15
Exodus 21:17

Chapter 19 Rejoice Always
    1 Thessalonians 5:16-18
    Philippians 4:4-7
    Ephesians 1:3-4
    Psalm 139:13-14
    Galatians 3:26
    Ephesians 2:4-9
    Romans 8:28
    Luke 6:27

Chapter 20 Where Do You Live?
    Matthew 6:7-13
    Matthew 6:7-13 (NKJV)
    Hebrews 13:7-9
    Romans 14:17
    1 Corinthians 4:20
    1 Corinthians 15:50
    Matthew 6:33
    Mark 10:15
    Luke 7:28
    Luke 9:62
    John 3:3-5
    Acts of the Apostles 14:22

Chapter 21 Seek Me First
- Zachariah 1:3
- Malachi 3:7
- Proverbs 8:17
- Jerimiah 29:12-13
- Amos 5:4

Chapter 22 Sorrow a Key Ingredient to Repentance
- 2 Corinthians 7:9-10

Chapter 23 Wake Up Church
- John 17:14-23
- 2 Chronicles 7:14

www.ingramcontent.com/pod-product-compliance
Lightning Source LLC
LaVergne TN
LVHW041332080426
835512LV00006B/414